THE HOWARD MIRACLE
JOHN CLARKE

JOHN CLARKE

THE HOWARD MIRACLE

INTERVIEWS FROM 'THE 7.30 REPORT'

TEXT PUBLISHING MELBOURNE AUSTRALIA

The Text Publishing Company
171 La Trobe Street
Melbourne Victoria 3000
Australia

This edition published 2003

Printed and bound by McPherson's Printing Group
Page design by Chong Weng-ho
Typeset in Stempel Garamond by J & M Typesetting

National Library of Australia
Cataloguing-in-Publication data:

Clarke, John, 1948- .
The Howard miracle : interviews from the 7.30 Report.

ISBN 1 877008 85 0.

1. Howard, John, 1939- - Interviews. 2. Politicians -
Australia - Interviews. 3. Australia - Politics and
government. I. Title.

320.994

CONTENTS

THE HON. JOHN HOWARD, PRIME MINISTER OF AUSTRALIA

Mr Howard, thanks for your time.

It's a great pleasure, Bryan, as always.

And congratulations.

Thank you very much.

Have you ever had a broad overview of your political philosophy turned into a book before?

Not to the extent that this current volume does it, I must say. I'm impressed.

It's pretty comprehensive, isn't it?

It's a very thorough collection indeed, yes. Your people have done an excellent job. What I like is that you've put a whole lot of other people in here as well. It's not just me.

That's right. I'm pleased you approve.

I think it's great. And it makes the book a unique record.

Quite agree. Also, there's a sense in which we might not see your greatness, if all we saw was you. And I hope you don't misunderstand me there.

Not at all. You need the contrast. I can see that.

Exactly. It also reflects the enormous influence you've had on the quality of argument in this country.

Yes. Look, I wonder if I might just thank the media in that regard.

By all means.

They have been terribly important in all this, you know.

Indeed they have, as emerges from the book, I think.

That's right.

And the book encapsulates a lot of history, when you think about it, doesn't it?

It does, and one of the reasons it's interesting to read is that, when the events described were actually happening, they were all just a blur.

I bet they were. Things are moving so fast these days aren't they?

My word they are.

Do you get much time to study analysis of what might be called 'the Howard method'?

Well, as a general rule we do everything to make sure that doesn't happen.

Analysis of how you go about your work and achieving your goals?

Yes, we're very dark on that sort of thing.

So this is really a 'first' then?

Oh, different 'institutes' have put out propaganda of various kinds, of course.

Gerard Henderson and so on?

Yes.

I meant anything genuinely analytical.

And I think, at its best, Sydney talk-back radio is an awfully good test of an idea.

Do you try policy ideas out on radio?

Oh yes. Many times.

And the results stand up to scrutiny pretty well, do they?

As I said, we try to make sure that doesn't happen.

But how do you prevent it?

It's not easy. Fortunately the Australian media are based in Sydney. And in the case of SBS and the ABC, of course, we own them.

And you've mounted an attack on the ABC, haven't you?

It's not so much an attack on the ABC as it is an examination of its finances.

That's clever.

It's not bad, is it? Responsible government. Concerned with public process. Must watch the budget and so on.

What have been the major achievements of your period in government, do you think?

Very hard to say. But one very important thing is that we've stayed in power.

Yes, you've really dominated, haven't you?

You can't do much if you're not in power. I'm a great believer in making sure you're still there at the end of the day.

How have you managed that?

Well, perhaps we should discuss this after you've read the exchanges in this book.

I look forward to that, and I can see you don't want to give too much away but there are patterns, aren't there? Consistencies in the way you've done things?

Like what?

Like, if there's good news you're always there. If someone wins something, some sporting thing, you're always there sharing their triumph.

I love sport. It's very Australian.

Exactly. The Bob Hawke thing. But if something bad happens, if there's bad economic news, when the health system is being destroyed, when education is being reconstructed as a two-tiered system, you disappear. Then suddenly there's an immigration crisis. Or the governor-general business is allowed to fester and fill the papers for months. Or you have an urgent trip to Washington. Or you wrap yourself in the flag and welcome some troops back from somewhere.

You seem to be suggesting these things are distractions.

I suppose I'm just thinking aloud. I wasn't meaning to sound critical. I'm trying to describe a pattern. You move things around well. You mix the bowling up, to use a cricketing metaphor.

I love cricket. I think all Australians love cricket.

That's another thing you do. You've tried to compress the definition of 'Australian'.

Do you think so? I'm not sure I agree. I just think it's obvious that an Australian is a white urban heterosexual Christian employer who loves sport.

That's my point.

Good. We agree then.

I suppose another example would be the sale of Telstra.

Another example of what?

Of mixing things up, of running the issue in what appears to be an

open way, but ensuring you get the result you want.

Let me say this. I am the prime minister. It's not an easy job. Sometimes I have to do things in a roundabout way to get the best result for the country.

For all Australians.

Yes. For all Australians.

It's what you think is best for the country, and how you go about securing that result, which interests me.

Is that building on fire incidentally?

Where?

Out the window. See the smoke?

Smoke? That's cloud, isn't it?

Is it? It looks like smoke. Is it nimbus? Strato-cumulus? Celsius or whatever that other one is? What's the other sort of cloud?

To finish the Telstra thing, Mr Howard, you want it to be privatised but the public is opposed to it. So what do you do?

You privatise part of it.

Exactly. You change the question. The question is no longer 'Would you like it to be privatised?' The question now is, 'Given that we've sold half of it, how do you feel about our selling off the rest of it?'

Privatisation is no longer the issue.

Exactly.

That building is definitely on fire.

Mr Howard, there isn't a building out there.

I've enjoyed our little chat. Let's talk again once you've read the book.

Thank you.

PART I
THE STRATEGY
1998–2000

THE HON. KIM BEAZLEY, LEADER OF THE OPPOSITION

In which the Opposition forms an orderly queue.

Mr Beazley, thanks for your time.
Good to see you, Bryan.
Had a good year?
I've had a very good year, yes. Enjoyed it a lot.
Lost an election?
Lost an election, yes, but at least we didn't win it.
That wouldn't have been good?
No, we'd be running the country now if we'd won it.
Didn't you want to run the country?
Oooh, no. Bad business, running the country.
You said you did before the election.
Well, you've got to say you want to run the country if you're standing in an election.
You'd have to say that, I suppose.
Yes, there's not much point in saying 'vote for us, we bat down to about number 3 and we've got the same policies as the other lot'.
Of course not. 'Vote for us, we don't want to be the government.'
No, you can't say that.
People wouldn't vote for you, would they?
No, they wouldn't. And they didn't.
It worked.
That's right. It was a completely successful campaign.
So what's next for you?
More of the same. We'll be opposing. The job of an opposition is to oppose.
But you're not opposing the people who run the country, are you?
Oh no, we're not crazy, there's no future in that. You're not going to get anywhere opposing the people who are actually in power.

Why not?
They're the popular ones. They're the ones with the public support.
So who are you opposing?
We're opposing the government.
How do you do that if you're not really opposed to what they're doing?
Well you *say* you're opposed to what they're doing.
Can you give me an example?
Yes, you say, 'We are opposed to all this economic rationalism.'
Because it has tossed hundreds of thousands of people out of work?
Yes. It exports jobs. Shifts control of the economy outside the country.
Removes the checks and balances?
It does. And it forces society to cannibalise itself.
You say all those things?
Yes.
But your policies don't depart much from economic rationalism.
No, they can't afford to.
Why not?
The people who run things might get annoyed.
Would they say so?
Oh, yes. You'd know all about it.
How?
The dollar would get a shagging. You wouldn't be able to afford a fridge or a lawnmower.
Society would fall apart.
It would be the end of the Westinghouse system.
Westminster system.
I beg your pardon. I used to know all this stuff.
You think we're seeing the collapse of the Westminster system?
I think under the Howard miracle, you won't even be able to get the parts...
Thanks for your time.
...But don't tell anyone I said that.

THE HON. ALEXANDER DOWNER, MINISTER FOR FOREIGN AFFAIRS

In which important distinctions are made.

Mr Downer, thanks for your time.
Delighted.

This is a disturbing development, isn't it, these attacks on Serbia?
These are not attacks on Serbia, they're attacks on Mr Milosevic.

Isn't Mr Milosevic in Serbia?
Yes, he is. That's why they're bombing the joint. He's the president.

So that's the reason Serbia is being attacked?
Serbia isn't being attacked. These are not attacks on Serbia, they're attacks on Mr Milosevic.

Do the Americans know the likely consequences?
Hang on a minute. It's Nato, not the Americans.

I see. Of course.
This is an important point. Let's be clear about the auspices here. This is a Nato operation.

And how do we know what Nato is doing?
We watch American television.

Do the Natovians know exactly where Mr Milosevic is?
I don't think they do, no.

So what are they bombing? You said these aren't attacks on Serbia.
I don't know *exactly* what they're bombing.

Do you know *roughly* what they're bombing?
Serbia. I've told you that.

They haven't told you what they're bombing?
Why would they tell Australia what they're bombing? We're not even in…

America…
Nato.

Why are you supporting them if you don't know what they're doing?
Something's got to be done about Mr Milosevic. He's killing people there.

Isn't Nato killing people up there?

These are not attacks on Serbia, they're attacks on Mr Milosevic.

Mr Downer, you've already said you don't know what they're doing.

What I've already said is that these are not attacks on Serbia, they're attacks on Mr Milosevic.

Will anyone else get hurt?

As I understand it, it will just be Mr Milosevic.

What if there's someone standing next to him?

You wouldn't want to be standing next to him. I would advise any Australians in the area...

But they'll wait till he's on his own, won't they?

As I understand it, yes.

Is this like the attacks on Iraq?

No, this is miles north. Serbia is well north of Iraq. It's in the former Yugoslavia.

Mr Downer, did the attacks on Iraq get rid of Saddam Hussein?

I haven't seen the paper today.

He's still the President of Iraq, isn't he?

I'd be speaking from memory.

Is he still killing people, Saddam Hussein?

The issue here is not Saddam Hussein.

Mr Downer, what's our role in Nato?

Australia's role?

Yes.

We don't have a role in Nato. We're not in Nato.

So why are we supporting these attacks on Serbia?

These are not attacks on Serbia, they're attacks on Mr Milosevic.

THE HON. JOHN HOWARD, PRIME MINISTER OF AUSTRALIA

In which a firm financial base is established for the job ahead.

Mr Howard, thanks for your time.

Pleasure.

You've made a number of statements lately about how well the economy is going.

It's performing brilliantly.

We've got growth.

We've got growth, we've got low interest rates, we've seen off the Asian crisis.

Pretty good result.

Pretty good? It's dazzling. The market is travelling well.

Commodities are in the dunny, aren't they?

They are. But bank stocks are very strong.

Yes. Why are they going up?

They're making a fortune.

Why?

Good management.

Really?

Yes, they've cut costs.

How?

They've fired thousands and thousands of people.

Is that a good thing?

In the view of the market, yes.

What about in your view?

I'm guided by the market in these matters.

But what about policy?

That is my policy. I have a look at the *Fin Review*. I'm pretty well informed.

What about a policy for the country?

For the whole country?

Yes.

The market's the best judge of what's going on in the market.

Why are there stock market crashes then?

That's most unusual.

Mr Howard, you said during the election that you would be working to create jobs for Australians.

Peter Reith's an Australian.

You said when the economy comes right, one of the great benefits would be in the creation of jobs.

Well, the economy is not quite that right.

How right is it?

The market part of it is going OK.

And the management part.

The CEO sections are moving well.

But not the part that affects the majority of Australians?

What do you mean, the majority?

The greater part of, the biggest number of.

The majority of Australians voted against us.

But you said you were going to govern for *all* Australians.

We'll, I've had a fair bit to do. I can't do everything.

What have you been doing?

I've been talking to the market. I'm the prime minister.

THE HON. BRIAN HARRADINE, INDEPENDENT SENATOR

In which useful intelligence information is gathered.

Senator Harradine, thanks for joining us.
Hello there.
Just before I ask you anything I want to get a couple of people on the line here. *(Picks up phone, speaks into it.)* **Is Beverly there, please?**
Who is Beverly?
BEV: Speaking.
Beverly Williamson?
BEV: Yes, that's right.
You voted for Senator Harradine?
BEV: Who?
Brian Harradine?
BEV: Is he the one with the ears?
Yes.
BEV: In the Senate?
That's right. You voted for him.
BEV: Yes.
Right. Stay on the line will you, Bev?
What are you trying to do here, Bryan?
Hang on a minute, Senator Harradine. *(Speaks into phone.)* **Hello? Dave Kirkland?**
BLOKE: No, hang on. You want Dave?
Yes, please.
BLOKE: He's just out the back moving the truck.
We'll wait if he's not going to be too long.
BLOKE: OK, hang on a minute.
What is all this, Bryan? What are you doing?
Well, I want to ask you about a Goods and Services Tax and I want to get the people who voted for you on the line.
BLOKE: Are you there?

Yes.

BLOKE: Look, can he call you back? He's just ducked away for a minute.

OK.

What are you doing, Bryan?

I want to ask you about the GST, Senator Harradine, and in case any issue comes up, you might like to talk to your electorate.

BEV: Hello?

Yes, Bev. We'll come to you in a moment. Hello?

BLOKE: Hello.

Dave Kirkland?

BLOKE: No. He's not back yet.

Well why are you on the line?

BLOKE: Weren't you looking for Dave Kirkland?

Yes.

BLOKE: Well, he's not back yet.

Did you vote for Brian Harradine?

BLOKE: No. Have you spoken to Bev Williamson?

Yes, I've got her on the line now.

BEV: Hello?

Hello, Bev?

BEV: Can I ask the audience, Eddie?

Hang on. We'll come back to you, Bev.

BEV: What are you doing?

We're looking for Dave Kirkland.

BEV: He's just gone past my place. He'll be home in about five minutes.

OK. We better kick off without him. Senator Harradine, even with only 50 per cent of your constituency on the line, are you happy to talk about a GST? Hello? Dave Kirkland?

BLOKE: No, he's not back yet, mate.

EDDIE MCGUIRE,
TELEVISION CELEBRITY

In which the troops are subjected to first-class entertainment.

Righto, mate, are you ready? Are you sitting comfortably?

Can you repeat the question, Eddie?

I haven't got to the question yet, mate. Calm down.

Sorry, Eddie, I'm a bit pumped.

I'm a bit pumped myself, mate.

It's pretty exciting, isn't it?

It's huge, mate. It is huge. Let's play. Righto, Bryan. First question, mate. Are you ready?

Can I have a lifeline, Eddie?

No, that's not the question, Bryan. You'll know the question because you'll be given four potential answers.

OK.

OK. First question, mate. What happens in this show?

A. You get asked hard questions?

B. You get asked easy questions?

C. You get asked hard questions for a while and then they get easier?

D. You get a couple of full tosses and then when we've got advertisers crawling all over each other, we get you to recite the periodic table in Urdu and toss you out and get someone else in?

All of them, Eddie.

No, you've got to pick one, ballbag. That's the game.

D.

Lock it in, mate?

Yes, Eddie.

Lock it in, matey-watey? Lock that little rippersnorter in? You're coining it now, mate. You have won $200. Jeez, you'll be out strapping one on with the boys tonight, won't you, shagger?

There may be some celebration at some stage, yes, but I haven't got far yet, Eddie.

Are the boys watching, mate?

Probably, Eddie.

I'll bet they are. And why wouldn't they be, ladies and gentlemen. The boys will be out there. What do they watch, mate? 'The Footy Show'? MMM footy broadcast? Masters golf? Big Kerry's cricket? They'd be into that, wouldn't they?

The boys are very catholic in their tastes, Eddie, yes.

I'll bloody bet they are, mate. Nervous? A bit nervous, are you?

I'm quietly confident, Eddie.

Right. Your next question. Who wrote Beethoven's Fifth Symphony? Was it

A. John Farnham?

B. Men at Work?

C. Beethoven?

D. Little Pattie?

Can I have the question again, Eddie?

Yes, mate. Who wrote Beethoven's Fifth Symphony. Was it

A. Sherbet?

B. Col Joye?

C. Beethoven?

D. The Man From Snowy River?

C, Eddie.

You are cooking with gas here, mate. Sporting question here, mate. You'd like a sporting question, wouldn't you, mate?

Yes, that'd be good, Eddie.

How many premierships have Collingwood won since the 'election' of their very dashing, prominent and successful president?

A. None?

B. Half?

C. The boys are very pumped up?

D. You wait till we get hold of those Dockers?

I'll play.

What time can you get there?

No, I mean I'll have a go at the question.

Fair enough.

A.

Let's have a look, mate. Mate. Mate, you have just won $800. How do you feel, mate?

Pretty good, Eddie.

What are you going to do with it all?

I'm going to pay my tax.

You're going to give it to Johnny Howard. It never stops does it, mate.

I actually owe them a bit more than that.

Good on you, mate. Now we'll just go to a break so we can win about 1.5 mill and then we'll come back and see how you go. You're going well, mate.

THE HON. PETER REITH, MINISTER FOR EMPLOYMENT AND WORKPLACE RELATIONS

In which some slight teething problems are sorted out.

Mr Reith, thanks for your time.

Good to be here.

Do you think John Howard's leadership might be in trouble?

No, no, John's got everyone's support.

Not the electorate's.

Not the electorate's, no, but all the important people are behind John.

I see you've released a statement about the government's position.

I haven't actually done that yet.

Have you got it with you?

(He pulls out a document.) This is it here, yes.

And this will be released later today?

Yes, it's gone to the papers. It'll be in the papers in the morning.

Would you like to read it?

I'd love to read it but I haven't got my glasses.

You can have my glasses.

Are you short-sighted?

No, long-sighted. Are you short-sighted?

Pathetically. Famously. I can't read this properly.

Have you got a copy of it? Because I can read and correct you if you go wrong.

Yes, we could have a try, if I go off the rails, just say so.

OK. Right. *(He reads, unsurely.)* 'The Reith government will...'

The Howard government. The second word there is 'Howard'.

Sorry, it does say 'Howard'. 'The Howard government is dedicated to performing the Austrian Rail-station system.'

'Reforming the Australian taxation system.'

I beg your pardon. 'It will continue to maximise disruption in the Australian workplace.'

'Increase productivity.'

Sorry. Miles away. 'And consequently will be continuing with its policy of class hatred.'

'Industrial reform…'

Good heavens.

Yes, you've jumped a line. You're down here.

I'm sorry. '…with an organised campaign of provoking Australians…'

'providing Australians…'

'…to despise one another as we…'

'to develop together…'

'…as we approach…', is that 'approach'?

Yes.

That's not bad, getting 'approach'.

No, you're doing well.

'…the twentieth century.'

'Twenty-first.'

I beg your pardon?

Wrong century.

'So I would sack…'

'say to…'

'So I would say to all you mongrels…'

'say to all Australians…'

'…we're after your arse…'

'…wherever you are…'

'…we'll get you.'

'…we wish you well.'

Sorry, how was the rest of it?

Spot on.

THE HON. JOHN HOWARD, PRIME MINISTER OF AUSTRALIA

In which an important alliance is forged.

Mr Howard, thanks for your time.
Pleasure.
You've been meeting with Meg Lees almost every day since we last spoke.
I have, yes.
And how has it gone?
Very well. What a nice person.
She is a nice person, isn't she?
It was most enjoyable.
What actually happened?
We sat down. We spoke in a general manner.
What did you say to her?
I explained that I was in a spot of bother. Needed a bit of a hand.
A bit of advice?
Yes. I ran it past her in broad outline.
How did you describe the problem?
I said I was running a democracy.
What did she say?
I tell you what, she's got a very good sense of humour.
Likes a laugh?
Oh, she's wicked.
Did you actually say you were running a democracy?
Yes.
Don't the people run a democracy?
And you reckon she didn't pick *that* up?
She's quick.
Doesn't miss a trick.
Did you explain what you'd done?
Yes. She asked me for a bit more information.

What did you tell her?
I said I'd brought in a policy people didn't want, without consulting them on the detail. And without having the numbers in the parliament.
Is this conversation recorded?
Yes. It's all official. There are minutes and so on.
Are there?
Yes. It's like Hansard. Here are the minutes from yesterday, I was just checking through them.
Can I have a look?
I don't see why not. I'm planning to be out of the country when the tax comes in.
(He reads.) **'The meeting began at 10.22.'**
It's good, isn't it? What does it say next?
'Mr Howard asked Meg Lees whether she had considered his offer.'
That's right.
'Ms Lees asked whether this was the same offer he had made a week previously and which had been rejected on approximately 312 separate occasions.'
'Mr Howard sought some guidance as to the precise number of times it was necessary to repeat a statement in fairly simple English in order for its delivery to be effective.'
'Ms Lees requested clarification as to whether or not perhaps there was some flannel or heavy towelling material impeding the passage of sound through Mr Howard's aural passages.'
'There was some speculation from Mr Howard as to Ms Lees' apparent incapacity to distinguish between the lower reaches of her torso and her elbow.'
'Ms Lees suggested a brief adjournment at this point which would provide Mr Howard with an opportunity to see an ophthalmologist.'
'In an attempt to break the deadlock Mr Howard ventured the opinion that it might be an excellent idea if Ms Lees were to avail herself of the education system and in particular the aspects of it whose job it is to accentuate the knowledge of the broader public in the area of economics.'

'Ms Lees asserted that this was a privilege already vouchsafed to her and she expressed some surprise that a detailed knowledge of macroeconomic reform in its many aspects was a part of the training normally available to small-minded suburban solicitors.'

'Mr Howard asked whether or not there was any point in continuing with this conversation, richly-textured and enlightening though it undoubtedly was.'

'Ms Lees concurred and suggested that should Mr Howard have a brief period over the next couple of hours when he wasn't being instructed what to do by big business or Treasury, he might like to go out into the street and see how much photochemical smog was being produced by diesel engines.'

'Mr Howard attempted to disavow Ms Lees of the view that he had arrived in conjunction with the previous shower.'

'Ms Lees named a prominent religious figure and offered a detailed suggestion about the exact placement of the GST as outlined.'

'It was agreed that the meeting would reconvene after lunch.'

What's this here about food?

That's just a note to myself, for our next meeting, to make sure we've got something to eat.

Why?

All through the meeting she wanted to get takeaway food.

Really?

Yes. Takeout food. She kept saying it over and over.

THE HON. JOHN HOWARD, PRIME MINISTER OF AUSTRALIA, AND THE HON. PETER COSTELLO, TREASURER

In which we are debriefed after a successful raid.

Mr Howard and Mr Costello, thank you both for your time today.
H: That's a great pleasure.
C: Good to be with you, Bryan.
Can I ask you about the deal you've done with Meg Lees?
H: It's all been announced.
C: What would you like to know about it?
Do you think it'll happen?
H: Yes, she fell for the whole thing. We pretended she talked us into some things we were going to do anyway. Hook, line and sinker.
C: She accepted it completely. Meg Lees has a fine understanding of the issues involved. She was a pleasure to work with.
Can she actually deliver the package?
H: She's got to.
C: She's finished if she doesn't.
What happens if she *does* deliver it?
H: She's finished.
C: Not our department, Bryan.
What happens if there's a rebellion in the Democrats?
H: Not very likely.
C: Have you ever seen the Democrats?
H: I think we'll be all right there.
C: Rebellion? These people are going flat-out to get a quorum.
There's talk of defections and there's obviously a great deal of dissatisfaction with Meg Lees' performance over this.
H: Not from us there isn't.
C: I think he means the Australian public don't want the deal.
H: Public? Who gives a fat rat's about the pu…

C: We cleaned her up, Bryan.

H: People have got to understand that we're trying to find a way of making the GST fair and equitable. *(Laughter.)*

If the GST was equitable you wouldn't have to make a whole lot of concessions to get it through the parliament, would you?

H: Good point. It wasn't equitable but it is now.

C: How can a consumption tax be equitable? It only taxes spending!

H: No, hang on. Shut up.

C: Sorry, Bryan.

But what are you going to do about the fact that the Australian public doesn't want this tax?

H: Not the bloody public again. Have you got any real questions?

C: Hang on. People can hear you. What makes you say they don't want it, Bryan?

The polls say 86 per cent are opposed to it.

H: There's only one poll that matters, Bryan.

C: We've got a mandate there. Got a mandate in the big one.

No you didn't.

H: I beg your pardon. We won the election.

C: You're wrong there, Bryan.

You won in the Reps but the public made sure you didn't have control in the Upper House.

H: Yes, but we fixed them up, didn't we!

C: Why do you think we've been duchessing Meg Lees?

But how can you make it work?

H: We're going to spend 28 million dollars on explaining why it's such a good idea and why we've got to have one.

C: A lot of money.

Twenty-eight million dollars?

H: Very important message.

C: It needs to be explained to people.

Where are you going to be spending the 28 million dollars?

H: In the media.

C: We're spending it in the Australian media.

Are the media for or against the GST?

H: Now or after we give them the 28 million dollars?

C: At the moment or once they get the cash?

After they get the money.

H: Hard to say.

C: Very difficult to say.

Do the public know you're spending 28 million dollars of their money?

H: It's not the public's money.

C: It's our money, Bryan.

H: Nothing to do with the public.

C: Jeez, I'm sick of the public.

Thanks for your time.

C: Thanks for *your* time.

H: Thanks for your money.

THE HON. TIM FISCHER, LEADER OF THE NATIONAL COUNTRY PARTY

In which the getaway vehicle is taken for a run.

Tim Fischer, thanks for your time.
Good to talk to you, Bryan.

You must have been pleased with the response to your decision to get out of politics.
Yes. I have been affected by the warmth of the response, yes, both from colleagues.

And from who else?
No. They were both from colleagues from memory.

You're being given a fair old send-off in the media, aren't you?
There are some very fine journalists in Australia. I think it's one of the things we do best.

Let's go back over some of the events of your time in politics, because it's been an interesting time, hasn't it?
It has. I wouldn't have missed it for quids.

You were elected in... what?
I was elected in New South Wales.

Yes. What year?
1999.

So how long were you in there?
I've got no idea. My watch is in the glovebox.

No, I'm asking about the period since you were first elected into parliament.
Oh yes, you're not allowed in if you're not elected, that's the way it works.

When was that?
Yes, no doubt about that at all.

Just reading from tomorrow's paper here...
I'm in tomorrow's paper?

There's very little else in it. It's mostly you, tomorrow's paper.

Did they use the photos?

Yes, here you are in the army…

Yes, that's me.

What's this here? This is you being a statesman, is it?

No, I'm just wearing a hat.

It says here 'Tim Fischer: The Statesman'.

That must be the car. I'm just standing there in a hat.

Here you are splitting the atom.

No, I'm just wearing a hat again. Here I am going for a swim, look. That's up the bush.

Yes 'Tim Fischer: The Great Australian' it says here.

Great Australian?

Yes.

That can't be right. I voted for a GST.

Here's one of you with a store dummy.

Where?

Here. You're showing an R. M. Williams store dummy a sheep.

That's John Howard.

No. That's a sheep.

This other one here. That's John Howard.

What's he looking like that for?

He's trying to look like an Australian.

Why?

He's going to bring in a GST.

Will you miss the cut and thrust? Do you think?

Two questions there.

Let's take the first one. Will you miss the cut and thrust?

No. I'm getting out before they introduce a GST.

But you helped bring it in.

Exactly. I'm not a complete idiot.

Well what's this then?

That's me in the hat again.

Mr Fischer, thanks for your time.

Gidday. I'm Tim Fischer. How are you?

THE HON. ROBERT HILL, MINISTER FOR THE ENVIRONMENT

In which significant achievements in the field are acknowledged.

Senator Hill, thanks for your time.
Very good to be here.
You must be pleased.
Yes, indeed.
To have Kakadu listed as a uranium mine.
It's a great result. We're very proud.
Good for Australia.
Australia didn't do it. *We* did it.
I mean it's good for Australia that it happened.
You've lost me.
Is it tough to get a site listed as a uranium mine?
Yes, it's quite a detailed process.
How do you do it?
First of all you've got to get elected.
How do you do that?
You adopt a lot of policies you think people will like.
Like what?
Like envirotuninal policies.
Environmental policies?
That's them.
You're the Minister for the Environment.
Of course I am. I just turned part of it into a uranium mine.
So you get into power with your environmental policies. And then what do you do?
You do what you like once you're in.
This is why we're increasing greenhouse gases?
Yes.
And turning a national park into a uranium mine?
Not the whole park.

A park with a uranium mine in it?

Yes. Nice big park. Few trees. Shrubs. Herbaceous borders.

And a uranium mine.

Australian industry at work.

You won't be able to drink the water.

Why not?

It'll be poisoned. That's what happens with a uranium mine.

The miners will take the water with them.

Is it a beautiful place?

Not really. It's a big hole in the ground full of trucks and bulldozers.

I mean Kakadu.

Kakadu? It is now, yes.

You don't think it always will be?

We've given an international undertaking to turn it into a uranium mine.

You've promised?

Solemnly.

Mr Hill, thanks for your time.

This is a Howard government promise.

THE HON. JEFF KENNETT, PREMIER OF VICTORIA

In which, sadly, one of the lads outruns his supplies and loses his way.

Mr Kennett, thanks for your time.
Good evening.
You've called an election.
For the eighteenth of September.
During the footy finals.
Yes, there'll be a show of hands at half-time in the preliminary final.
And you're confident?
I hope I'm not over-confident. There's always a chance something will go wrong in this type of thing.
In an election?
Anything where people are given a choice, yes.
There's always a chance they'll get it wrong?
There is, sadly, yes. Mistakes happen. They've happened before.
They have. You're spending 24 million dollars on education.
No, we're not.
If you get in.
If we get in we will, yes. We're certainly not doing it at the moment.
Have you got the money?
Are you kidding? The economic management of this state is probably the best in the country at the moment.
Things are going well?
We're rolling in it. Haven't you seen the accounts? We've been rolling in it for years.
Why aren't you spending 24 million dollars on education at the moment then?
We will if we get back in.
It's needed, is it?
Yes, the education system in Victoria is falling apart.
Why?

I forget why.

Bad teaching perhaps?

No. Can't be that.

Why not?

We fired the teachers.

How's the health system going?

You've lost me. The expression 'health system'?

Back to education then. Why haven't you done something about it?

We're going to.

If you get back in.

I can't do anything about it if we don't.

But if you've got the money, why don't you do it now?

Are you reading the questions properly?

No, I threw away the questions you gave me.

What are you reading now?

I wrote my own questions.

That's smart. Where were you educated?

I was educated before you got in.

THE HON. JOHN HOWARD, PRIME MINISTER OF AUSTRALIA

In which the enemy is completely outfoxed.

Mr Howard, thanks for your time.

Good to be here. Thank you.

I'd like to talk to you about the constitutional referendum tomorrow.

No, you'll have to do it now. I can't come back tomorrow. We've got a referendum on tomorrow.

Just a few questions.

As long as you're not asking me which way I'm going to vote.

You're going to vote against it.

I know. I just don't want everyone to know that.

Why not? You've been opposed to it from the beginning.

It's a secret ballot.

What do you think is going to happen?

I don't know. It's a very exciting time for Australia.

Why do you say that?

This is the first new idea we've had in this country for a while.

I suppose it is, yes.

And it's great to be part of it, isn't it?

Great to be part of what?

Great to be part of making sure it doesn't happen.

Don't most people want Australia to become a republic?

I didn't say it was easy.

Why do you think it's not going to get up?

Well, the people are being asked to vote for a model they don't want, aren't they?

And they don't seem to like the people who are running the republican argument?

I think they see that in many cases they're the people who would normally be lobbying for the job of governor-general.

So why was that model the one that was put to the people?

That's what the prime minister decided.

But the prime minister is a monarchist.

Look, the monarchists are travelling OK at this point. We've got a model the people don't want, run by people they don't want running it. And we've got a preamble as well.

What's the point of the preamble?

Oh, mix the bowling up a bit.

I mean constitutionally.

No point constitutionally. It's got no meaning. It's not binding. Have we got a preamble in the current constitution?

I don't know.

There you go.

People don't know whether the preamble is part of the republic vote or part of the proposed model or what.

If they're not sure they should vote 'no'.

Not sure about what?

Not sure about anything.

Whether or not they've left the gas on.

They should vote 'no' if they're not sure.

Is Peter Reith really a republican?

Peter Reith is a dangerous radical, yes. He's a direct election republican.

Why?

We drew straws. He got that one.

Thanks for your time and good luck with it all.

Don't need it.

THE HON. MICHAEL KNIGHT, NSW MINISTER FOR THE OLYMPICS AND ROADS

In which we are privileged to witness greatness.

Mr Knight, thank you for your time.
It's a pleasure.
On this new ticketing crisis…
I wouldn't call it a crisis.
What would you call it?
It's an issue, certainly.
How would you describe the issue?
A cock-up with the ticketing arrangements.
You've changed the basis on which people can get the tickets they want.
No, no, can I stop you there? We don't want people getting the idea they can somehow get hold of the tickets they want. What we've established up to this point is that that's what you can't do.
You can't get the tickets you want? What can you get then?
People can get tickets to the Olympics, but they can't get the tickets they want.
And they should put in for those now.
Oh yes, I'd be quick.
They're in great demand.
No, the tickets people want are in great demand.
What about the tickets they don't want?
They're being supplied.
Supply and demand.
Separate concepts.
It must be hard to see so many people so disappointed?
In retrospect we shouldn't have asked people what they wanted.
That's the trouble, you think?

Well, you wouldn't ask people to put in for concert tickets and then let them say on their application what they'd like to hear sung.

Is the position completely hopeless?

Not if we can get Ian Thorpe to take up archery.

Cathy Freeman?

If we can get Cath involved in some of the early rounds of the dressage.

And the wrestling?

No. You leave SOCOG to me.

Mr Knight, where are the people who are going to the Olympics going to stay?

That's a stupid question, because obviously they've got to make accommodation arrangements of their own.

It's not a stupid question because where are they going to stay if the hotels are all booked out?

It is a stupid question because how could anyone possibly know the answer?

It's not a stupid question because at the moment they're saying every hotel in Sydney is completely booked out for the whole period of the Games.

It is a stupid question because if that's the position, that's the position.

It's not a stupid question if you'll be able to make a booking just before the Games for about twice the cost of a hotel room now.

Are you suggesting that hotels would say they'd sold out now so they can control the supply of accommodation and get the price up, and then suddenly find they have got rooms when the Games are on, but they're a lot more expensive than they are now?

Yes.

You're suggesting that these people would engage in exploitation. That they would have no interest in this whole business other than what they themselves could make out of it?

Yes.

Is that what you're suggesting?

That's right.

Don't prevaricate. Is that what you're suggesting?

Yes, that's what I'm suggesting.

It's a simple enough question. Is that what you're suggesting?

Yes it is.

I give up. If you're not going to give me a straight answer I can't help you.

PROFESSOR DAVID FLINT, CHAIR OF THE AUSTRALIAN BROADCASTING AUTHORITY

In which greatness is once more thrust upon us.

Professor Flint, thanks for your time.
Good evening.
You're the head of the Australian Bank Marketing Board.
No, I'm the head of the Australian Broadcasting Authority.
I beg your pardon.
That's OK.
What's the difference?
The Broadcasting Authority supervises the maintenance of standards in broadcasting.
The maintenance of what?
The maintenance of standards in broadcasting.
Standards in broadcasting?
Yes.
In Australia?
That's right.
And when are they coming in?
They exist now. They've existed for many years. We're in charge of them.
How much do you charge for them?
We don't *charge for* them. We're in *charge of* them. You don't buy them. They are not a commodity.
Sorry, what are they exactly?
They're guidelines which govern the behaviour of broadcasters.
Like, for example, what aren't they allowed to do?
They're not permitted to start a nuclear war, for example.
What about a limited nuclear war?
They're specifically precluded from starting a nuclear war of any kind.

Are they allowed to bring down governments?

Yes. I think if, in their view, a government isn't performing they could bring it down.

Could they criticise the sort of people who own radio stations?

That would depend on the owners of the station. That would be a matter of station policy.

Could they criticise the sort of people who don't own radio stations?

Give me an example.

Well, could they criticise the unemployed and the disadvantaged?

Again, that would depend on the owners of the station.

If it were OK with the station owners, though?

Provided it was OK with the people who owned the station, yes.

Provided no-one was paying you to say those things?

That's right. Or not to say the opposite.

Yes.

Or to refrain from denying that the opposite of the opposite was the case.

Yes. Or the other way round.

Yes, or to have entered into some arrangement whereby the audience was given the impression that the views expressed in the program were those of the person speaking.

Except in those cases where the person speaking was being paid to say those things?

Yes that would be legitimate, provided that it was clearly the case.

Nothing secret?

No.

Why not?

Not telling.

Professor Flint, thanks for your time.

Would it be possible to get a cup of tea?

THE HON. JOHN HOWARD, PRIME MINISTER OF AUSTRALIA

In which things are clarified to very good effect.

Mr Howard, thanks for your time.
A great pleasure, Bryan.

You've met with the New Zealand prime minister, Helen Clark?
I have, yes, we had very fruitful talks.

There are differences, of course?
Yes, there are indeed. She's a woman.

I mean in terms of policy.
That's right. As I say, she's a woman.

Can you explain the problem with the defence alliance?
The New Zealand government wants to scale back its defence commitments. They've decided not to proceed with the purchase of a new frigate, for example.

Why?
They haven't got any money. They can't afford it.

That's no good.
The problem is it leaves a gap in the pattern of regional defence.

Why haven't they got any money?
In New Zealand?

Yes.
They've got a completely market-driven economy in New Zealand.

Isn't that what we want to have here?
We'd do it better. They've sold everything off, they don't even own their own infrastructure anymore.

What have they sold off?
They've sold the lot, the telephone system…

Like selling Telstra?
No, that's a good idea. But imagine doing it in New Zealand.

What else have they sold?
They've sold the power, the gas, you name it.

Isn't that what we want to do?

It'll be different here.

How?

It'll work here, trust me.

Haven't they reduced taxation rates for business and lowered the top personal rates?

They have, yes. They've done very well.

How have they paid for that?

They've sucked a lot of money out of the rest of the community.

How have they done that?

They brought in a GST.

If they're creaming money off the top of every transaction, why haven't they got any money?

I don't know. Maybe they didn't do it the right way.

But isn't that what we want to do?

They've done it badly.

Can't they undo it?

How would they do that?

Can't they buy those things back and get the country to run properly the way it used to?

I don't know. But the point is they haven't got any money.

Why not?

I don't know but I was very interested to talk to the New Zealand prime minister.

Why?

Because it's exactly what we're going to do here.

THE HON. BRONWYN BISHOP, MINISTER FOR AGED CARE

In which our enterprise is blessed by genuine concern.

Bronwyn Bishop, thanks for your time.

What a pleasure it is.

I wonder if I can talk to you about your performance over this nursing homes issue?

It's not just my performance, Kerry. I have a whole department of other people who don't know what's going on either.

I'm not Kerry, I'm Bryan.

If you'll let me finish, Kerry. The fact remains that I am simply the minister. I'm simply the minister responsible. None of this is my fault.

Minister, are you satisfied with the standard of care in Australian nursing homes at the moment?

I'm satisfied with it in some cases and not in others.

Can you be more specific?

Yes, I'm satisfied with it in the case of those nursing homes I've never heard of but I'm a great deal less satisfied with it in the case of the ones I've managed to find out anything about.

Are you happy with the performance of your department?

Look, it's a very hard job.

What is?

Whatever it is they're supposed to do. It's tough. I couldn't do it.

How do you know that?

I don't even *understand* it. These people have got to *do* it.

What do you take 'ministerial responsibility' to mean?

I'm not here to discuss theory, Kerry. There's not much point in that at this time. We've got a lot of older people in some of these places.

We have to do something about the standard of care, don't we?

This is a very practical problem. Let's work out a solution. What the minister has got to do is get in there and *fix* it.

You *are* the minister.

Exactly. Let's get on with it. As soon as those facts are presented to me I'll be on the case like a ton of bricks.

How will you do that?

We will look at any complaint as soon as we are made aware of it.

How would you be made aware of a complaint?

Someone would write to us.

They have.

Historically, yes, but just let me finish, Kerry. They would write to us, documenting the nature of the complaint and detailing the facts involved.

And then you would act?

Hang on, Kerry…

…Bryan.

Hang on, Kerry, you've asked me a question. No, we would not act yet.

I'm sorry. What would happen next?

The letter would be referred to the right people.

Who would it be referred to?

I don't know who is involved but that would take approximately three months.

And then the letter comes back?

Not always, no.

But sometimes.

On the odd occasion, yes, the letter might come back.

And then you would know about it?

Not necessarily.

Why not?

We mightn't be there when it came back.

Why wouldn't you be there?

I could be anywhere. I might be in the parliament. I might be out looking at a nursing home. The standard of aged care in this country is a disgrace!

Can it be improved?

It has to be. These people can't look after themselves, some of them have worked all their lives, served their country overseas, raised families. It's very important that we let these people have their dignity.

How will you do that?

I'll round up some television cameras and visit a few of them.

Thank you, minister.

You may touch my raiment, Kerry, but only briefly.

THE HON. JOHN HOWARD, PRIME MINISTER OF AUSTRALIA

In which there is some minor confusion about the seating arrangements.

Mr Howard, thanks for your time.

Good evening, very good to be with you.

Mr Howard, how many policies do you have on Aboriginal affairs?

Do you mean in town or in the bush?

Let's look at the 'in town' ones first.

In the city, or in the regional centres?

In the cities.

In an election year or just normally?

All the time, ideally.

An all-the-time, work-for-all-cases Aboriginal policy?

Yes.

I'm afraid I don't understand your question.

Let me put it this way. Can you explain the business of mandatory sentencing?

Certainly. Do you know what mandatory sentencing is?

No, that's what I want to ask you.

OK. Do you know what 'mandatory' means?

It means obligatory.

What does obligatory mean?

Obligatory?

Is it Irish?

Not O'Bligatory. Obligatory.

Where is it? Is it up in the Territory?

It's a bit like 'unavoidable'.

Ah yes. Mighty pretty country round there. I was up there recently.

You were in the Northern Territory?

No, but I was up that way.

Where were you?

I had to go up to Pymble for a meeting.

Mr Howard, why is the United Nations being critical of Australia at the moment?

I don't know. I've been trying to work that out. This has got nothing to do with the United Nations.

What hasn't?

The treatment of Aboriginal people in Australia.

The UN has said they haven't got basic human rights.

The UN has got no business criticising us at all.

Why not?

Because we support them. We helped write their human rights charter.

They have a human rights charter?

Yes, the member countries of the United Nations formed a charter years ago.

Are we a member of the UN?

A very important member. Doc Evatt wrote a fair bit of the UN charter.

And what is the purpose of the UN human rights policy?

To prevent governments from acting in a way which would threaten the lives of their own citizens.

Would that happen?

It has. Look at East Timor.

That was tragic, wasn't it?

Sometimes a government is so bad, so bereft of what the broader world would accept as a basic standard of moral responsibility to its own citizens…

…that it will simply ignore the plight and condition of sections of its own people?

Yes.

And what might happen?

Many of them will die.

So the UN seeks to protect the fundamental human rights of those people?

That's the idea.

And if it doesn't, who will?
Exactly. If the UN doesn't say something about the condition of these people, their privations and their distress might continue.
These are genuinely appalling governments you're talking about, aren't they?
They are. I'm citing the extreme to highlight the UN policy and its importance.
So what is our objection to the UN's criticism of us on this issue?
It's none of their business when it happens here in Australia.
Do you mean 'What right do they have to speak about what's going on in an individual country?'
I do. We're running Australia. The United Nations isn't running a country.
Doesn't it represent all the countries?
Yes, but there's a difference between what you'd like to happen and what actually happens in the real world. It's like going to church. You go to church on a Sunday, you listen to a lot of stuff about what you ought to do, how you ought to live your life…
You agree.
Yes, you agree. That's why you've gone to church.
But you don't act on the principles you've expressed your support for.
No, you wouldn't need to go to church if you lived like that anyway. You'd be out there doing it.
So what is Australia's position on human rights? We support the UN charter on human rights?
We support the UN charter on human rights, but we are opposed to the UN charter on human rights.
Hang on, Mr Howard. You can't say that. It doesn't make sense.
Doesn't it? Are you sure?
You just said, 'We support the UN charter on human rights, but we're opposed to the UN charter on human rights.'
I see. I can't be on both sides.
That's right. It doesn't make sense. Do you want to answer the question again?

Yes. Ask me again.

Mr Howard, do we support the UN charter on human rights?

In theory, yes.

But not in practice.

We support it in practice in Timor.

But not south of Timor.

No.

We support in the Gulf.

But not in the Gulf of Carpentaria.

Do we support it in the Falklands?

Yes, but not in the other rural electorates.

THE HON. MARK VAILE, MINISTER FOR TRADE

In which we attend to matters of detail. Quiet please. This is important.

Mark Vaile, thanks for your time.

It's a pleasure. *(To the dog.)* Get in the truck.

Pardon?

Talking to the dog. *(To the dog.)* Sit down.

Mr Vaile.

How are you? A bit of weather about, isn't there?

Yes. You are Australia's trade minister.

Are you the bloke with the canola seed?

No, I'm Bryan.

What do you want? Did you have a price in mind?

I'm Bryan Dawe.

(To the dog.) Sit down.

You're Australia's trade minister.

Listen, I couldn't look at it till Tuesday. We've got a big lot of stock coming in from Deniliquin in the morning. I've got superphosphate from Armidale to Broadford stacked all over the joint up home and I've got two of my best blokes out with the flu.

But you've accepted the job as trade minister.

I have but I've told the bloke there…

Howard.

I don't know, some mate of John Anderson's, I've told him I'll just have to get there when I can. *(To the dog.)* Get in the bloody truck.

Why didn't you take the job the first time it was offered?

I thought John was going to take it. That'd normally be the way we'd work it. This used to be Tim's job. You get the car, the unlimited kilometres…

…the phone.

Yes. Tim throws a seven and gets out, Ando's in.

Why didn't he want it?

Don't know, mate. I've been out the back of Young for a week and a half with 4000 hoggets and we belted the diff open on the first day.

If John Anderson took over the leadership of the party, wouldn't he normally become the trade minister as well?

Look, it's a funny year. Everything's different this year.

Well, who's Warren Truss?

Warren is a bloke from Queensland. He's more your sugar man.

Why is he the Minister for Agriculture and Fisheries?

He must be a mate of Ando's. I used to be in that job. That's not a bad job. You can phone that one in.

Are you aware there's a storm brewing with the Canadians over salmon imports?

I'm on the case. We've got a couple of hundred old two-tooths to finish crutching and then I'll be up there arguing the toss with those Canadians quick as look at you.

Did you need much convincing to take on the Trade job?

No. Just took a couple of days to get hold of me.

Good luck with the portfolio.

(To the dog.) Sit down.

THE HON. MICHAEL WOOLDRIDGE, MINISTER FOR HEALTH

In which the distinction between standard equipment and a luxury item is shown to be gender-based.

Dr Wooldridge, thanks for your time.
Nice to see you. Sit down. What seems to be the trouble?

You've created a bit of a furore with your remarks about tampons, which attract the GST because they are, of course, a luxury item.
Yes, well, I've apologised for my remarks.

Why did you apologise?
I got told to. John Howard rang and told me to apologise.

Why did he say you had to apologise?
Apparently I'd upset a whole lot of people.

Who were they?
I don't know. Some minority interest group somewhere.

Women?
That's it. That was them, yes. I don't know who's organising them.

You don't know who women are?
Yes. I know who women are. I'm a doctor.

You're trained to tell the difference.
Oh yes, it's one of the first things you learn.

But you didn't recognise them as a political grouping?
I didn't realise they were working together, no.

I don't think they were, were they? Until you united them.
I've provided them with a point on which they all agree?

Yes.
That's certainly the thrust of a lot of the e-mails we've been getting.

That you're a little p…?
Yes. That I'm just a little patronising.

Have you done it before?
The tampon routine, 'I beg your pardon, I didn't know menstruation was a disease.'

Yes. The comparison with shaving cream.
Oh, I've done it plenty of times. I'm a doctor. It normally works pretty well.

It's pretty funny, isn't it?
I think it's funny, yes, and as I say it normally goes gang busters.

Who is your normal audience?
I'm a doctor.

So mostly blokes.
Yes. And a lot of women who want to marry doctors.

They'd find it funny.
Oh. They are the greatest audience.

They'd pick up everything I suppose would they, the women?
Not if they look after themselves they won't.

How are they going to look after themselves?
Yes, we're getting a lot of e-mails about that.

THE HON. JOHN HOWARD, PRIME MINISTER OF AUSTRALIA

In which bonding with the troops is seen as a crucial adjunct to iron discipline.

Mr Howard, thanks for your time.

Nice to be with you.

How are they hanging?

I beg your pardon?

How are they hanging? Nice sort of day, is it, up there?

What are you talking about?

Are you getting any rain up there at the moment?

Rain? Up here? I don't understand what you're talking about.

Mr Howard, I thought you were trying to appeal to the people in the bush. I thought that was your purpose in doing the interview.

'Appeal to people in the bush'?

Yes, I'm trying to help you appeal to the people in the bush.

Look. Why don't you just conduct the interview the way you normally would conduct the interview?

Mr Howard, you've got about five minutes to appeal to the bush or they'll never trust you again.

Don't patronise me, young man.

You won't even win Lane Cove in the next election, the way you're going.

Don't tell me my business.

I'm not telling you your business, Mr Howard.

I've spent most of this week in the bush, for your information. I don't know whether you know what's going on in this country.

You didn't, Mr Howard. You visited a few regional centres.

Yes, in the bush. That's where I've been. That's where the regional centres are.

That's not the bush.

I assure you we were in the bush. Somebody saw an echidna.

An echidna?

Yes. You can't even get a decent hotel in some of these joints. Don't tell me we weren't in the bush.

Mr Howard, listen. You can't simply put on an Akubra, fly into these small towns and expect people to vote for you.

Did you see the coverage we got in the *Sydney Morning Herald*?

Well, there's your problem.

We got more media than you can shake a stick at.

Mr Howard, there is your problem. This is the mistake made by the Keating government and the Kennett government.

What are you saying? I don't understand what you're saying.

You've got to appeal to the bush. It is imperative for your survival. And if you're going to do that, we can't conduct the interviews the same way.

How are we going to conduct it then? What do you suggest I say?

(Bryan hands him a piece of paper.)

Read that. OK? We'll start again.

Read this? What? Now?

No, no, no. Once we get going. Just follow me at the start, OK?

Certainly.

Right, here we go. Mr Howard, thanks for your time.

Nice to be with you. Thank you.

How are they hanging?

(Reads.) 'They're hanging very nicely, thank you.'

Getting your share?

'I believe my share is in hand, yes, thank you.'

Ah, terrific. Mr Howard, what are your three most important policy initiatives?

Over what time frame, young man?

By tonight. Now read that.

By tonight? You're joking! *(Reads.)* 'By tonight we will abolish the GST...'

Good.

'We will also buy Telstra back—and have a look at the question of tariffs from the point of view of the *Australian* economy rather than from the point of view of the *American* economy.'

Good. Now say goodbye.

Why say goodbye?

Just in case the horse has bolted.

THE HON. PETER COSTELLO, TREASURER OF AUSTRALIA

In which new technology is revealed essentially to be very simple.

Mr Costello, thank you for your time.
It's a pleasure.

Can you explain why so many Australians are buying shares at the moment?
Oh, they'll bet on anything, won't they? The greatest gamblers in the world, Australians.

Sorry, Mr Costello. We're actually broadcasting.
I beg your pardon? We've started?

Yes.
Sorry. Can we go again?

Yes, sure. Mr Costello, thanks for your time.
Good evening, Bryan. You have an investment question, I understand?

Can you explain why so many Australians are buying shares at the moment?
A lot of people want a future in this country, Bryan, and a lot of people want a stake in that future. And there are some very sensible super-annuation provisions which people are taking advantage of.

Why now, particularly?
The economy is going so well, a lot of people want to participate in that vital growth.

And where is that growth coming from?
What I mean by that is Australian companies are increasing in value.

How do we know that?
You look at their market capitalisation. It's going up.

How can you tell?
You look at the market, you see what their stock's worth.

Why is the market so high at the moment?
Because a lot of people want to buy the stock.

Well, hang on. They're buying shares because the market's going through the roof and the market's going through the roof because they're buying shares?

That's the way it works. It's pretty rational, Bryan, the market.

And what are they buying?

At the moment they're mostly buying the tech stocks and investing in what's called the 'new economy'.

And how does this new economy differ from the old economy?

It differs in that it doesn't exist.

Why are people investing in it if it doesn't really exist?

Because they think perhaps at some future time it might come into existence.

They want to get in on the ground floor?

Yes, or possibly the roof garden. It's a bit hard to tell. There's an awful lot of guesswork…there's a lot of gam…there's a lot of bet…there's a lot of very solid work being done by equities advisers in the investment market.

So what are people looking for in these stocks? A dividend?

No, they're not going to get a dividend off the tech stocks at this stage, are they?

Do they require, then, an expert valuation?

An expert valuation, yes. Or a whisper from a cab driver or a natter with a bloke in a fruit shop. Anything will do, Bryan.

And where are they getting the money to invest in these companies?

They're selling stock in other companies they've invested in.

The old economy ones with the dividends.

The solid ones, yes.

Wouldn't that mean that those stocks are undervalued?

Well spotted.

So people are selling high-quality, solid-yield stocks and buying tech stocks?

Yes. Anything dot com. Anything telco.

Anything they don't know.

They often know the company because a third of Australia's junior mining companies, for example, have in the last six months become internet service providers, so they often know their names.

There'd be huge demand for the internet stocks.

There is.

Is this based on any sort of business fundamentals?

No, it's based on the demand for internet stocks.

Demand is based on itself?

Yes, and there are more stocks coming on the market all the time. I've got a report here about what's expected to happen next week, for example.

Like what?

Race 4, No. 5, Dotcom.

Race 5, No. 2, Telco.

Race 7, No. 12, Bloke Told A Mate Of Mine.

Mr Costello, thanks for your time.

Thanksforyourtime.com. That's a very good idea, son. Write that down. We can float that.

THE HON. RICHARD ALSTON, MINISTER FOR COMMUNICATIONS, INFORMATION TECHNOLOGY AND THE ARTS

In which we hear from a very clever communications expert.

Senator Alston, thanks for your time.
Very nice to be with you.
What's the trouble with Telstra?
It depends on who you're talking to.
I'm talking to you. What do you think?
Well, it depends on who I'm talking to.
You're talking to me.
Well, it depends on what you ask.
I'm asking you what the problem is with Telstra.
Well, it depends on how well I'm talking.
Who to?
Exactly. It depends on who's there, doesn't it?
OK. Let's say we're talking to the market.
Oh, if I'm talking to the market, I'd say that, tragically, Telstra doesn't
work terribly well as a private company because the majority
shareholding is owned by the government. It's hobbled.
And you're going to sell the rest of it?
We're still talking to the market?
You are.
Of course we are, yes. I think everybody knows we're going to tip the
lot out at some point, yes.
And if you're talking to the electorate?
We're not going to sell any if I'm talking to the electorate, no!
You're not going to privatise the whole of Telstra?
(Violin music plays in the background.) No, we hold the national
telephony infrastructure in sacred trust for all the people of Australia.
A great institution was built up using the tax monies of ordinary

Australians and the backbreaking and selfless work of a great many people in the bush, and we hold that in sacred trust. *(Violin music stops.)*

Minister, what does partial privatisation mean if you're talking to the market?

It means we're going to sell all of it, but we're going to do it in bits.

Sell it all off, but in stages?

Yes. We can't sell it all in one go. Someone might notice we were doing it.

There's not enough money to buy it all in one go, is there?

That's the other point. We let a little bit go and we say, 'We're never going to do this again, you'd better be in.'

'Hurry, hurry.'

Pardon?

'Hurry, hurry.'

We're going like the clappers, son, I assure you. We are moving as fast as we...

I mean, that's your catchcry? 'Hurry, hurry'?

(Violin music plays again.) Our catchcry is that we hold in sacred trust for the people, particularly in the bush, the national telephony infrastructure. *(Violin music stops.)*

But it doesn't work as a government department, does it? You've just fired 15,000 people.

I beg your pardon? I haven't fired anybody.

Well, no. Telstra did.

Oh, Telstra may have, yes.

Did you think it was a good idea?

As the minister or as a private citizen?

As the minister.

I was appalled as the minister, obviously.

What about as a private citizen?

I thought it was inevitable, given the costs position. A bold decision, well-executed.

Minister, did you know they were going to fire 15,000 people?

As the minister or as a private citizen?

As the minister.

Yes. They told me that.

And what did you say?

I said, 'It's a good thing I'm not here personally, boys. I could get very snaky about some of this stuff. I'm actually the minister.'

Did you get back to yourself?

No, I've got a message bank. I'll do that later.

On the broader issue though, Senator, what is the public's difficulty with selling the whole thing?

Well, look at the history of Telstra. This is a difficult issue for a lot of people. We put a phone line into your house in about 1947.

Yes, which I paid for.

Which you paid for, using your taxes.

And then you charged me rent for it.

Of course, yes. We charged you a nominal fee for rental.

And then you charged me to connect it.

There's a connection fee, yes.

And then if I made any phone calls, you charged on every call.

You've got to pay for your calls, that's reasonable.

Not much of an arrangement, Senator.

It's an excellent arrangement and if you didn't like it, of course—

There was nothing I could do about it.

It was a monopoly. There was nothing you could do about it.

It must have been one of the most successful businesses in the world.

I don't think I've ever known of a single service being paid for quite so many times in the history of commerce, no.

And what happened to it?

Well, this is where John Howard's a genius, of course. *(Clears throat.)* He sold it.

He what?

He sold it.

What did he do that for?

It was a goldmine. He's very clever and he found a way of selling it to the people who already owned it.

Why would you buy something you already owned?

I often wonder that myself. It's one of the great mysteries how we got away with it.

And we still get charged for our phone calls?

Of course. What's more, you voted for us because we said we were going to do it.

That is fantastic, isn't it? Senator Alston, thank you very much for your time.

(Quietly.) Sacredtrust.com. That's not a bad idea.

I beg your pardon?

No, sorry, miles away. *(To someone off-screen.)* Is the car here?

MR KEVAN GOSPER,
IOC VICE PRESIDENT

In which we see the value of carefully thought-out judgment.

Mr Gosper, thanks for your time again.
Thank you for inviting me in.
**Mr Gosper, you're in a bit of trouble over this business of your
daughter carrying the Olympic torch, aren't you?**
I don't know that I could have done a great deal about this.
You could have declined the invitation.
This invitation was not issued from here, it was issued by the Greek
Olympic people.
You could have declined the invitation.
I don't really know what else I could have done.
You could have declined the invitation.
As a consequence of what's happened, of course, we're now in a
position where an eleven-year-old girl is likely to be subjected to
suspicion and to abuse in the schoolyard.
You could have declined the invitation.
Obviously, that's not a fair thing. And I think it's fair to consider her
position. She's had to give up school and go to Europe to do this. She's
missed an awful lot of school.
You could have declined the invitation.
In fact, I've even seen it mentioned that I might have engineered this. I
don't know what sort of evidence there is for that.
You could have declined the invitation.
Just because I'm working at the IOC and my daughter's having a little
bit of a run on the ball with the flame…
You could have declined the invitation.
…I don't think it's reasonable. I don't see how anybody can assume for
one moment that there's anything suspect about the way these things
were organised.
You could have declined the invitation.

I just don't see what else I could have done.

You could have declined the invitation.

Unless, of course, people are thinking that there's something objectionable in my having gone to Greece with her. What was I supposed to do?

You could have declined the invitation.

I just don't know what else I could have done.

You could have declined the invitation.

It's a bit difficult to imagine what else I could have arranged.

You could have declined the invitation.

The good thing about it was at least we got to spend some quality family time together. That's a very difficult thing to do for me, of course, because I'm invited overseas so often.

You could have declined the invitation.

I do object, though, to having to come in here on programs like this and defend my reputation against attacks of this kind.

You could have declined the invitation, Mr Gosper. Thank you very much for your time.

PART II
THE DIVERSIONARY PHASE
2000-2001

THE HON. PETER COSTELLO, TREASURER OF AUSTRALIA

In which we see how vital it is to get the message across.

Mr Costello, thanks for your time.
Thank you for inviting me in.

Nice to see you again. How are things going?
Pretty good, I think.

Are you looking forward to the GST?
Oh, yes, the boys are pretty pumped up.

You think it will go well?
We'll be happy to come away with a win. Very happy with the four points.

Because it's going to be a real thrill for a lot of people, isn't it?
Oh, undoubtedly. It will be an absolute career highlight for a great many citizens here.

I'm really enjoying the ads, I have to say.
The ads? The ones on television? The ones with the chains falling off people?

Yes.
We're very happy with those. They're going gang busters, aren't they?

Yes. What do they mean?
They mean that when the GST comes in, people will be freed from…

Chains?
Well, no, the chains really are a metaphor.

What are they a metaphor for?
They're a metaphor for the taxes that will be coming off people when the new taxes go on them.

Mr Costello, did you think of having the chains come off to then be replaced by other chains?
Other chains representing the new taxes?

Yes. They'd be a metaphor.
Look, I really don't want to take a black armband view of accountancy.

We did think of alluding to the new tax but unfortunately there wasn't time. It's a great idea, but we simply didn't have the time.

You decided to go just with the chains coming off?

Yes.

No thought of a big hammer coming down on top of everyone?

No. As I say, we thought about it but decided against it. There was another one where there was a big rug whipped out from underneath everybody.

You didn't like that one?

Personally I thought it was terrific. And it had very, very strong visuals, but...

Didn't fit the time?

Sadly, again, just that lack of time, that telltale lack of time.

Mr Costello, do bank fees attract the GST?

No, they're exempt. Why do you ask?

Because I see bank charges have gone up 35 per cent in two years. Are you telling me the government is not making any money out of this at all?

Not as such.

But it's not good for the public, is it? A 35 per cent increase in charges?

Hang on. Be fair here. We can't be responsible for the public. We're the government. We've got important government projects on.

What have you been doing?

We've been making all these ads with the chains falling off people.

And tell me. Do the poor get poorer?

Oh, yes, that's a bit of a feature, I think you'll find, if you read your history.

I mean in the ads?

No, certainly not in the ads, no.

And are the rich laughing?

No, why would the rich be laughing?

In the ads? Aren't they laughing?

No, they're not laughing. Why?

Haven't they got the chains coming off them?

No, the people with the chains falling off them have mostly got overalls and they drive trucks and they're called Bevan, and so on.

What are the rich doing?

Well, who do you think made the ads?

I see.

I think you're going to have to repeat a year. Perhaps we'll discuss this later.

Mr Costello, thank you very much for your time.

When you've finished your homework.

THE HON. JOHN HOWARD, PRIME MINISTER OF AUSTRALIA

In which a golden opportunity is missed.

Mr Howard, thanks for your time.

Well, very nice to be with you, thank you.

I wonder if I could ask you about the huge turnout for Corroboree 2000?

Yes, certainly. What was the name of the team again?

Corroboree 2000. You know, the reconciliation movement, the walk across the bridge?

Ah, yes, I recall something of the type.

Did the enormous response surprise you?

No, not really. I'm speaking from memory…I think I spoke at it, didn't I?

Yes, you did. You had the opportunity to apologise too, didn't you?

This was the thing where a whole lot of people were given the wrong map.

A faulty map?

Yes, they were obviously under the impression I was going to be giving a speech from the rear of the hall. They were all facing the wrong way. Every time I looked up…

They had their backs to you?

All I could see were the backs of people's heads and lots of hats.

Maybe the acoustics were bad?

Frankly, I didn't like the look of any of them.

Mr Howard, did you see the speech as an opportunity to offer an apology?

I saw the speech as an opportunity to express some concerns I think a lot of people have about apologising for something that they didn't do.

But the apology that's required isn't about your personal responsibility for what happened.

That's good, because I haven't done anything wrong.

Isn't what's required, Mr Howard, an acknowledgment that what happened did happen?

Well, look, if something happened, obviously somebody did it. And it wasn't me!

You don't have to be the one who did something to feel sorrow for the people it happened to.

Good, OK, can we talk about something else now? Much though I have enjoyed the thrust of your early questions.

Mr Howard, you recently went to the battlefields of France?

I did, yes. I visited a number of Australian graves and…

You said you were sorry that they'd lost their lives.

It was a tragic loss of life, absolutely tragic.

Did you kill them?

I beg your pardon?

Did you kill them?

No, of course I didn't kill them. What do you mean, 'Did I kill them?'

How can you be sorry for something you didn't do?

Oh, this is completely different.

Why is it different, Mr Howard?

Well, you yourself said this was in France. It's not even in Australia. It's a completely different country. It's off the coast somewhere.

Do you think anyone actually agrees with you on this issue? There were a lot of people on the Sydney Harbour Bridge.

Plenty of people agree with me.

Who?

Well, look, my wife's brother works with a woman whose husband is a mechanic at a hospital. The person who runs the hospital, his sister knows a bloke who agrees with every aspect of what I say about this really rather complex question.

Can we ring him?

Certainly, we can ring him. I was talking to him earlier.

And he agrees…

He agrees absolutely with everything I say.

OK, it's ringing.

(*Howard's phone rings.*) Excuse me for a moment. Hello?

Hello. Mr Howard.

Yes, can I ring you back, mate? I'm just doing an interview. (*He hangs up.*)

Who was that?

I don't know, but don't worry about him.

Why not?

The GST'll get him.

AN EMPLOYEE OF THE AIRLINE INDUSTRY

In which it is conceded that the benefits of competition have been postponed.

Thanks for your time. *(Repeats.)* **Thanks for your time.**

I beg your pardon, you'll have to speak up. I work in the airline industry.

You are with the airlines.

Yes, I know. Have been for many years.

Which one are you with?

I'm with one of the big two. Everyone's with one of the big two. Everyone in the country. There's nowhere else to go. You've got to be with one of them.

Well, which one are you with?

Have you got one in mind?

Yes.

I'm with the other one. I joined them upon leaving school and I've gone rather well since.

It's a very competitive industry, isn't it?

The airline industry in Australia is very, very competitive indeed. We no longer have the two-airline policy.

What was the two-airline policy?

That was an arrangement whereby, if you missed one plane, you could be happy in the knowledge that had you got there a few minutes earlier you would have missed the other one.

Oh, yes. They still have that.

They've still got that?

Yes.

It's a very, very competitive industry.

Does your airline have frequent flyer points?

You'll have to speak up, I'm afraid. I work in the airline industry.

Does your airline have frequent flyer points?

Lashings of them. It's a major incentive scheme of ours, yes.

But you're in a bit of trouble, aren't you, about the conditions under

which you can use them?

We are at the moment, yes, but that'll blow over.

According to the rules, when *can't* you use frequent flyer points?

You can't use them at any time you wish to travel.

Any time you'd want to go anywhere.

That's right.

If there were, say, a special event.

Christmas?

Yes, Christmas, New Year, Easter.

You couldn't use your frequent flyers then, no. They're all excellent examples…

You can't use them when anything's happening.

That's right.

A footy final, Mardi Gras.

Anything of that kind. All 'no go' areas.

So when can you travel?

You can travel at any time when you don't want to go anywhere under any circumstances.

When you've got no reason to travel?

When you can't even think of anywhere you would be interested in going.

When it makes absolutely no sense at all to go anywhere?

The more pointless, the better it fits the regulations, yes.

So what is this scheme?

I'm sorry? I can hardly hear you. I work in the airline industry.

What exactly is this scheme?

It's an arrangement whereby we get rid of a whole lot of seats we can't sell.

No, I mean what is it called? Its technical name?

In marketing terms, it's an incentive arrangement for our very valued customers.

(Ding Dong!) **Whoops, there's my flight.**

No, son, I think you'll find that's mine. *(Ding Dong!)*

Are you sure?

You'll have to speak up, I work in the airline industry.

THE HON. ALEXANDER DOWNER, MINISTER FOR FOREIGN AFFAIRS

In which Noddy meets a most disagreeable person.

Mr Downer, thank you very much for joining us again.

It's very nice to be here again and thank you for inviting me.

It's a pleasure. Are you happy with events in Fiji this week?

I'm a great deal happier with events in Fiji this week than I was with events in Fiji last week.

George Speight has been arrested, I see.

Yes, it looks very much as if George's rather arrogant period in self-appointed government may have come to a sticky end.

You said you didn't approve of the idea of George Speight being a member of the Fijian government.

Dreadful fellow.

You actually said at one stage that he was 'beneath contempt'.

Beneath contempt—did I say that?

Yes, you did.

That's rather elegant, isn't it? Rather happily phrased.

You also said Australia wouldn't be happy with any government that contained a terrorist.

That's right. Imagine approving of a government that contained a terrorist. That's a shocking idea. It wouldn't just be Australia that wouldn't tolerate a thing of that kind. There'd be a great many other boys in the school who—

Countries in the region.

Sorry, countries in the region which would not tolerate such an idea. Terrorists in a government—what an appalling idea.

Does Australia have any dealings with any countries with governments involving terrorists? There's a list of them here.

Certainly not. Let's have a look at the list. No. None of these. We used to be a colony of that one.

But we aren't anymore?

No. This is an old list. Rhodesia. That doesn't exist anymore. That's called Zimbabwe.

Do we have anything to do with Zimbabwe?

In that case, yes, of course, we do have quite a lot to do with it. Yes that one, yes, yes, yes, no, not that one there, not that other one.

What's that one?

The Ross Dependency.

That's not a country, Mr Downer.

What's your point about these countries, young man?

I'm trying to establish which of these countries have had governments that include terrorists.

Terrorists or tourists?

Terrorists.

Terrorists. What an alarming idea.

You'd be less worried about tourists?

Oh, I don't think it's a bad thing for a government to contain tourists, no. The current government contains a great many tourists.

Does it?

Yes. It's led by a tourist.

And it still works, does it?

Well, you've got off the point a little bit there. I'd stick to the stuff about the terrorists and the tourists, if I were you.

I'm terribly sorry, Mr Downer, thank you very much.

'Beneath contempt'. That's rather good. I like that.

THE HON. JOHN HOWARD, PRIME MINISTER OF AUSTRALIA

In which the story of Canute is re-enacted for our amusement.

Mr Howard, thank you for your time again.
Good evening.
Mr Howard, are you going to amend the legislation on sexual discrimination?
Yes, we are.
Isn't that an area where the states have legislative control?
It is.
I thought you were opposed, as a federal government, to overriding the states?
We *are* in the instance of mandatory sentencing, of course, but not on this issue.
The issue of IVF treatment?
That's right. In-vitro fertilisation. 'In vitro' simply means 'in glass'.
Oh, so they do it in a test tube?
No, you can't do it in a test tube. A test tube's rather a small thing. As a general rule you need room to take your hat off.
I meant the fertilisation takes place in the test tube.
Oh, I beg your pardon, yes. That's all done by people in white coats.
So what is the issue here, Mr Howard?
The issue is quite simply this: who has access to IVF treatment?
And who has the right to stop them?
That's right. Somebody's got to stop them.
Aren't there already decision-making criteria in place to cover these questions?
There are, but I don't agree with them and I'm going to change them.
Mr Howard, didn't the court decide that your criteria were sexually discriminatory?
They did. That's right. That's why I'm going to change the rules.
Who's going to have access to IVF treatment under your legislation?

Women who are married.

Or are pretending to be married?

Yes, that'd do.

Or behaving as if they're married?

Yes, with any luck.

Women who'd like to be married?

Yes, girls with a few brains.

Not single women and gay people?

No, that's what I'm not having! I'm not having that. I'M NOT HAVING THAT!

OK, Mr Howard, settle down. Can I just throw a couple of other groups at you?

If you must.

Married child molesters?

No. Child molesters will not have access to IVF treatment.

What if you don't know they're child molesters?

In that case, how can you prevent them?

What about people who are living together when they get the IVF but not afterwards?

That would be unfortunate, but it'd probably be all right.

How would they get the IVF back if you didn't approve?

Exactly. You can't.

What would you do to them?

Oh, I don't know. Jail the mother?

What about people who don't like their children?

Are they married?

Yes.

No problem there.

You said a child within our society had a right to the care and affection of both mother and father.

I did, yes. That is my belief.

How are you going to make that happen?

In the case where there's only one parent you can't, obviously.

What about the case of two parents?

Well, you can't, again, obviously. Those are the only two areas, though, where that argument has any weakness at all.

What about a tree?

A married tree, this is?

Yes, a married tree.

Yes, no problem there. That should be OK.

Sheep?

Married sheep, these are?

Yes.

That can be very successful. This proposal went pretty well in Cabinet, for example.

What happened?

I told them it wasn't a matter for their conscience and they were to get through the gate quick-smart.

Mr Howard, thank you.

(Scribbles.) Thank you. Here you go. Any chemist will make that up.

THE HON. JOHN HOWARD, PRIME MINISTER OF AUSTRALIA

In which we see the same thing again and again and again.

Mr Howard, thank you very much for joining us.
It's a great pleasure and good evening.
And are you enjoying the Olympics?
Oh, what a fabulous spectacle. It's possibly the greatest single thing
I've ever seen.
The weather is beautiful, isn't it?
We've been very lucky with the weather. I hope it holds.
What did you think of the opening ceremony?
I thought the opening ceremony was a bit short.
You'd have preferred it to go on longer?
I felt it did go on, but that perhaps it could have gone on for longer. I
thought it was an absolute triumph of the—what's that thing where
you make stuff up?
Imagination?
Exactly. A triumph of that. In fact, I don't know where those people
who designed the opening ceremony are the rest of the time.
Well, they mostly work in the arts.
Do they? I thought they were Australians.
Yes, they work in the arts in Australia.
Where?
In the arts, Mr Howard. The arts.
Yes, so you say.
**Mr Howard, how are you going personally? You're turning up
everywhere and getting photographed.**
I've gone pretty well in the first week and I'm through to the semis.
You had an interrupted preparation, didn't you?
I did, I had a difficult preparation. I was photographed a great deal in
the first part of the year.
Anzac Day and so on?

Yes. Then I had a very dry patch in the middle of the year. I was barely photographed at all.

When the GST came in?

Barely photographed at all. Couldn't take a trick.

But you came back, as champions always do.

I put some hard yards in being photographed all over the place just before the Olympics.

And you couldn't have had a better first week if you tried, could you?

A dream run, a fantastic week.

Where are you standing?

The idea is to stand next to someone who's actually involved in sport and try and get your photograph taken.

But where are you standing in the competition?

I'm lying first. After the qualifiers, I'm lying first.

Really? Where have you been photographed so far?

I've been photographed at the swimming, at that thing outside where they go 'pull!' and then there's a kind of a pink explosion out in the air.

Shooting.

Is that what that is? I've been photographed out there.

The archery.

What's the archery?

It's the one where you fire an arrow into the target.

Oh, the Robin Hood stuff.

That's right.

Photographed out there, yes, with somebody's mother. The equestrian.

The which?

Equestrian. With the horses. Where I get in the R. M. Williams gear.

Well, Mr Howard, on behalf of all Australians, good luck.

Thanks, and it's great to know you're all there for me and I'm getting the hero faxes and thanks very much.

Terrific. How's the dollar?

(*Hums 'Advance Australia Fair'.*)

Why is Telstra firing 4000 people?

Sing, you fool.

AN EDITOR OF A METROPOLITAN DAILY NEWSPAPER

In which the quality of the press is explained, an unidentified source said today.

Thanks for your time.

Very nice to be with you.

You're the editor of a major metropolitan daily newspaper?

That's right.

Can I ask you why you've given this Peter Reith story such prominence?

It's not just us who's given it prominence. It's been given prominence across the board, in all of the metropolitan dailies and in the weeklies.

Yes, I realise that. Can I ask you why?

Well, it's a pretty important story, isn't it?

In what way?

Peter Reith has a phone and he let someone else use it.

Why is the matter still dominating the headlines?

Because statements have been made that conflict with earlier versions of the story.

These are statements that have been made by 'X'?

That's right.

Who's 'X'?

I believe X is a friend of Peter's son.

And X says she was given the phone card by Mr Reith's son?

Yes, and there's some suggestion that X may have been the person who gave the phone card to 'Y'.

'Y'?

I imagine he wanted to make a phone call.

No, I mean who is 'Y'?

A friend of X.

Did X actually give it to Y?

That has yet to be determined.

Maybe the card was simply found.

Who are you suggesting might have done that?

Y.

Because I'm a bit concerned about your line of questioning here. I'm not sure…Look, Peter Reith is a Cabinet minister. Have you read the story at all? It's a pretty important story.

But why is it a front-page story for three weeks? Imagine if everybody did that.

Everybody does do that. You fail to understand me. Peter Reith is the Minister for Workplace Relations.

Yes, but you didn't hop into him when he was cleaning the waterfront a couple of years ago and it went off.

No. But this story is completely different. It involves a telephone.

How is it different?

Couldn't be more different.

Because it involves a telephone?

Yes. It's much easier for people to relate to a story involving a telephone. How are you going to explain the nature and character of waterfront reform to people?

Shouldn't it be explained?

I've got no idea. I'm running a newspaper here. I'm not a reference library.

Why are people so interested in Peter Reith's phone card?

There are two reasons for that. Peter Reith made a mistake, a serious political error. He himself admitted that he made a mistake.

That's right, so why keep hammering it?

Reason number two is that no-one can stand Peter Reith.

Even so, why is it such a huge story?

You know his wife's got a phone as well?

His wife has a telephone? Have you also listed all the other MPs' wives who've got phones?

No. I'm running a newspaper here. I'm not running a reference library.

My point is the Middle East is exploding…

We did the Middle East! We already did the Middle East! I quote: 'Mid-East Peace Talks Explode Into Violence Shock'. It was on page 19, under Boat Trailers for Hire.

And what about the salination report?

The what? That's not a name I know. I'd be happy to look it up. What did he write his report on?

(Sighs.) **What about the economy?**

We've been doing the economy all week. 'GST Drives CPI to 10-year High Shock'.

On page four?

Well, we can't put it on page one, can we?

Why not?

What are we going to do with 'Peter Reith Toughs Out Phone Card Crisis: PM Stands By His Man'?

Is there no other news?

If there were other news, it would be in here! This is a *news* paper!

There must be something else going on.

Oh, there's plenty going on. Look. Page 2. We've got 'Cathy's Special Moment'.

What does the headline mean?

It means we've got a photograph of Cathy Freeman.

Have you got a photograph of Peter Reith?

Not in green lycra we haven't, son. If we did I think he'd have to resign. We'd call on him immediately to resign.

Why?

I've got no idea. I'm running a newspaper here. I'm not running a bloody reference library.

Thanks for your time.

MR JONATHAN SHIER, MANAGING DIRECTOR OF THE ABC

In which the national broadcaster is seen to be going through a bit of a purple patch.

Mr Shier, thanks for your time.
Can I thank you for inviting me on the program? It's very good to be here, and I thank you and the team for the invitation.
It's a pleasure. There's been a lot of discussion about the ABC recently.
There has, yes. This is a good thing. I think this speaks very well of us as a nation.
Why?
The ABC is a public broadcaster. It's owned by the public. I think it's good to see them taking an active interest in the ABC and in its workings. Of course the public use it.
Do they use it?
Oh, yes, the ABC is very well used by the Australian public. Every week the vast majority of Australians make some use, in one form or another, of the national broadcaster.
It must be a great privilege to run it then?
It is. It's a great honour. It's an honour of which I've been extremely conscious since my appointment. I regard it as an enormous privilege.
Have you worked in public broadcasting before?
Prior to this appointment?
Yes.
No.
What aspects of broadcasting have you worked in?
Previously?
Yes.
All aspects.
Have you worked, for example, in rural broadcasting?
With the possible exception of rural broadcasting.
Have you worked in news?

And news.

Current affairs broadcasting?

And current affairs broadcasting.

Have you worked in drama?

And drama.

What about sport?

Sport, I love sport. All Australians love sport. I think sport is a unifying theme in the national character.

Have you worked in sports broadcasting?

I've watched it.

But have you ever done any actual work in it, as such?

Directly?

Yes.

No.

OK. What about the weather? Have you ever done a weather report?

Paradoxically, no.

Make-up and wardrobe?

Have I ever done make-up and wardrobe?

Yes.

Personally?

Yes.

No.

OK. What about comedy? Have you ever done comedy?

Intentionally?

Yes.

No.

Have you ever made any television programs at all?

For a living?

Yes.

No.

What about *not* for a living?

Have I made a television program at home?

Yes.

Just to see if I could do it?

Yes.

No.

Mr Shier, what is your current position?

I'm currently the chief executive with the Australian Broadcasting Corporation.

Thank you for your time.

You're fired.

THE HON. KIM BEAZLEY, LEADER OF THE OPPOSITION

In which Australian success is seen to occur at every level internationally.

Mr Beazley, thanks for your time.
Rollback. Rollback. Rollback. Rollback. Pardon?

Mr Beazley, thank you for your time.
Rollback.

No. You say, 'It's a pleasure.'
Oh, I beg your pardon. 'It's a pleasure.'

Mr Beazley, thanks for your time.
Hello there. Nice to talk to you.

First of all, Kim, congratulations.
Thank you, very, very much indeed.

You must be pretty excited, aren't you?
I am excited, I'm thrilled. This is the thrill of a lifetime.

If anyone had told you last year you'd be up for an award...
I wouldn't have believed them.

You've literally come from nowhere, haven't you?
Yes. I just did bit parts all last year. I couldn't get a decent role last year.

Of course. And then you did *How the West Was Won*.
That is right. Had a lead in that. Had a wonderful time doing that.

That was really the beginning, wasn't it?
I think it probably was.

And then you did that touring one in the bus in the backblocks?
The road movie?

Yes. What was that called again?
Every Which Way But Policy.

With the orang-utan?
With the orang-utan, with me in the cab, yes.

Tremendous, yes. Where did you get that orang-utan from?
He was an office bearer somewhere in the New South Wales

Right with nothing better to do.

And then you did the one with Pauline Hanson.

In Queensland?

Yes.

Yes, *The Sting*. Pauline and I did *The Sting* in Queensland.

Yes, the Beattie picture. And I understand you're about to go away and do *Revenge of the Killer Tomatoes*?

No, unfortunately that's fallen through.

I thought you were up for that.

I was up for it, yes, but I didn't get the part.

Really? Is it still happening? Who's doing it?

John Howard's doing it. They're already shooting.

Who's doing the other part? The Won Nay Shon part?

That's all done with computer animation.

John Howard will need to be a bit careful there, won't he?

He will, yes. But he's done it before. He was terrific in *Crouching Hanson, Hidden Thumping*. Have you seen that?

I have. I thought he was very, very special.

He's pretty good, isn't he?

It's a fantastic film.

It's a very authoritative performance, isn't it? And a very different role for him.

He's normally so straight. Has he ever done this sort of action-comedy before?

Well, have you ever seen him walking in sports clothing in a foreign capital?

I meant in a film.

No, fair point. I don't think he has done it in a film before.

And the effects are great, aren't they?

Spectacular effects.

I love the way he seems to go backwards all the time.

Exactly, yes. All these other characters come into shot and go forward and John Howard goes backwards. It's amazing.

It must be awfully hard.

Technically it must be a nightmare. I was talking to the producer the other day. Apparently it's kind of a computer thing.

Right. So, Kim, tell us what else have you got on the drawing board?

Actually there's something pretty exciting next, I hope.

Great! What is it?

I'm going to do a thing called *Rollback*.

Great title!

It is a great title, isn't it. Fantastic title, *Rollback*.

What's it all about?

I've got no idea.

Really? Why did you decide to do it?

It's a good role, a very strong, important, principled role.

And a good title.

Great title, fantastic title—*Rollback*.

Have you read the script, Kim?

No, the script's not written yet.

So you don't know what it's about?

Well, I imagine it's about rollback.

What does that mean?

I've got no idea.

Do you have a synopsis?

What they told me is it's about a man who says he's going to roll something back, but nobody's quite sure what that means.

And you're playing the lead, the man, are you?

I'm playing the man, yes. They just told me to lose some weight and see if I could make some sense.

Best of luck, Kim.

(Sings.) 'Roll 'em in, roll 'em out, roll 'em up, roll 'em back…'

No, no, Kim, that's *Rawhide*.

Oh, I think it could get a lot worse than that, son.

THE HON. JOHN HOWARD,
PRIME MINISTER OF AUSTRALIA

In which we try to be as understanding as possible at this difficult time.

Mr Howard, thanks for your time.
Oh, good evening. Nice to be with you.
I wonder if I could ask you about the collapse of One.Tel?
Yes, indeed, a very interesting issue, this.
Let me get this right—you're supporting the union's case for redundancy payments.
I certainly am. What you've got here is a company that was run, frankly, by a couple of cowboys.
This is James Packer and Lachlan Murdoch?
No, no. They didn't run One.Tel.
They were on the board.
They were on the board. But they weren't aware of what was going on with the company.
Why wouldn't they know what was going on in the company if they were on the board?
I don't know. They didn't explain that to me.
Are they on the board of many companies?
Look, I'd rather get on and discuss one or two other things. But there are a number of very plausible reasons why James Packer and Lachlan Murdoch could be on the board of a company without knowing the detail of what was going on with the company.
What reasons?
They may have attended board meetings, for example, during periods of temporary deafness.
Temporary deafness caused by what?
Oh, a number of things—deep-sea diving. They could have spent many years in the artillery.
But couldn't they read the board papers?
Perhaps there were important, significant elements of the information

about the financial position of One.Tel which didn't reach them.

Why not?

There may have been a postal strike or something.

There hasn't been a postal strike.

Perhaps they attended the board meeting, fully equipped and prepared to speak, but were positioned in an inauspicious point of vantage. Behind a pillar or something.

And couldn't see?

And couldn't see! Exactly! There may have been a lot of glare.

What, off the pillar?

Indeed. Yes. Pillar glare.

Mr Howard, why are you helping the union and workers?

As I have said for a number of years, and my record is very clear on this, I believe that Australians deserve a fair go. I think that's a very Australian thing. I think this is one of the things that makes this such a great country.

You are John Howard, aren't you?

Yes, of course, I'm John Howard.

Do you have any identification on you at all?

I have my parliamentary ID. *(He hands it over.)*

That'll do.

Of course I'm John Howard. You asked me to come in here and I came in.

(He reads from the ID.) **It says you're John Howard.**

Of course it does. I am John Howard.

Married.

That's right.

Industrial relations activist.

That's right.

Are you familiar with the name Peter Reith?

Peter Reith, Peter...not a name I know, no.

Can I ask you to look at this photograph?

Never seen him before in my life, Your Honour.

Do you have a brother Stan?

Righto, that's it—

Is he involved in this company?

Everybody out, all the union members, out in the carpark. Now!

Mr Howard, what for? What are you doing?

Fire drill!

Fire drill?

Fire drill, very important.

Where's the fire?

Don't worry about the fire. I'll start the fire. Get out. You'll get burnt.

Fire drill!

Mr Howard, there's no fire.

Fire drill!

Mr Howard?

(Bryan is extinguished.)

THE HON. PHILIP RUDDOCK, MINISTER FOR IMMIGRATION AND MULTICULTURAL AND INDIGENOUS AFFAIRS

In which we get lost in a fog and have to radio for help.

Mr Ruddock, thank you for your time.
Good evening. Nice to be with you.
Mr Ruddock, are you happy with the way Australia is handling the refugee problem?
Yes I am. Australia's record in handling this problem, and let me also speak broadly of the generality of our record on human rights, is an enviable one.
Hang on. Sorry, Mr Ruddock. Can I ask you a technical question here?
Yes, by all means.
Why are they rioting and setting fire to the camps out in the desert?
What must be appreciated is that there are many, many thousands of people who, quite logically, want to migrate to this country. *(Phone rings.)* Many of them are in desperate positions in the country…
(Bryan picks up phone.)
(To Philip Ruddock.) **Hang on.** *(Speaks into the receiver.)* **Oh, hi.**
…in which they were born…
(Continues speaking into receiver.) **Oh, no, no, no, I'll meet you there.**
…so they quite rationally want to come here.
Oh, because I won't get time to get to both. No, I'll meet you at the Gresham, about 8.30.
There are two ways of doing this. You can do this legally. You can go through…
Nothing much. I'm interviewing Philip Ruddock.
…or in some of these…
No, it's going pretty well.
…some of these unfortunate cases…

He's talking about Australia's human rights record.

…where unscrupulous persons….

Don't know. Hang on, I'll have a listen.

…are exploiting these people shamelessly and in my view, trading in human misery. That's what they're doing.

I think he's against it.

…let me say that Australians have got to understand this, that…

Good point. Hang on, I'll ask him. Hang on a sec.

…we get in this country…

Mr Ruddock? Hello? Mr Ruddock?

Yes?

Aren't we blaming the victims? If refugees are being exploited by these unscrupulous operators, why are we putting them in jail when they arrive here?

Yes, that's a good question. Let me say in answer to that question, and I repeat…

(Speaks into receiver.) **He's going to answer it now.**

…going back to the generality of our record. Have a look at our record in the context of international measurements of human rights.

I don't know. Very hard to tell.

Our record is excellent. We have nothing to be ashamed of in this country.

I've got no idea. Switch on the television. We're on now, yes, yes.

We are a very good people. We are famous throughout the world for being a very good people.

Yes, that's me there.

And we're going to have millions of people trying to get into this country…

Yes, that's him.

…and they see detention centres catching fire…

He'll be here forever. I'll try to finish him up. Hang on, I'll wind him up.

…this is simply Australia's democracy at its very best…

Mr Ruddock?

…and visible in the public forum.

Yes? Thank you very much.

Oh, very good. Thank you for a very stimulating debate.

Yes. Thank you very much.

I enjoyed it enormously.

THE HON. ROBERT HILL, MINISTER FOR THE ENVIRONMENT

In which we come to understand the mysteries of the outside world.

Senator Hill, thanks for your time again.
Very nice to be with you. Thank you for inviting me.
There have been calls from the Queensland Nationals for you to resign.
I know. It's a difficult issue the environment, of course. It divides the community.
Into what?
Into the principally urban, relatively educated, largely bourgeois people who understand the broad issues, and the other lot of primeval thickheads. Incidentally, does this go to Queensland?
This broadcast?
Yes.
Yes. It goes right across the country.
Yes. On the other hand there are a lot of thickheads who live in the big cities and who think they know everything and who don't appreciate the valuable work done in the elimination of trees and the delivery of a scorched-earth policy up in the bush.
Sure. Senator, I wonder if you could explain Australia's position on the environment to us.
The global environment?
Yes.
I can. In fact, there was a huge international conference on just this issue.
This was in Kyoto?
No. No. This was up in Japan.
Sorry?
All the countries were represented and the scientific detail was astonishing. A great deal of evidence was provided to the conference.
Is the position serious?

With global warming?

Yes.

It'd make the nails fall straight out of your shoes, son. It's shocking. That's why the governments of the world were joining together to discuss this. But structurally there's a problem. The gases that cause all this environmental damage are not produced by governments.

They'd be caused by industry, wouldn't they?

Quite right. But the disadvantage doesn't accrue only to the businesses that produce the gases.

No. The effects are felt by everyone.

Exactly so. Hence the role of governments.

Representing the people.

Correct.

So what happened in Kyoto?

I'm sorry I can only tell what happened at the conference I went to in Japan.

Well, what happened there?

The countries of the world, broadly speaking, agreed to reduce their production of greenhouse gases.

Great. Did they all agree to this?

All, with the exception of two.

Two countries refused to do that. Who were they?

They were the US and Australia.

What did they want?

They wanted to increase their production of greenhouse gases.

Increase the production of gases that are causing the greenhouse problem?

Yes, that's right.

Hang on. This will cause damage to more than those two countries, won't it?

Yes.

So why did the US and Australia agree to that?

I'm sorry. I can only talk about the decision of the Australian government.

OK. Why did we decide it?

Because we were told to.

Who told us to do that?

The coal industry. Australia's greatest export is coal.

But, Senator, shouldn't we be creating new industries because of this problem?

We don't need new industries in this country, sonny. We're doing very nicely, thank you.

Why?

We sell a lot of coal.

Do we or do we not agree with the principle of reducing greenhouse gases?

Don't worry about the principles. It's not going to be ratified.

Why not?

Because the US is the greatest producer of greenhouse gases and they're not going to bloody sign it.

Senator, are you with the Australian government or the US government?

Technically?

Yes.

Technically, I'm with the Australian government.

Senator, thanks for your time.

I'm the Minister for the Environment.

Yes, sure.

Except if this goes to Queensland.

THE HON. TONY ABBOTT, MINISTER FOR WORKPLACE RELATIONS

In which the heir apparent tries a few range-finders.

Mr Abbott, thanks for your time.
It's a great pleasure.
Mr Abbott, I wonder if you could explain what's happening in this country at the moment to do with workers' entitlements?
Yes, I can. Funny idea, isn't it?
What is?
'Workers' entitlements.' It's an amusing concept.
Oh really? Why do you say that?
I would have thought if you wanted entitlements, the last thing you would do in this country is become a worker, but that's maybe just me.
What are you saying? That it's a contradiction in terms?
I'm saying it's not a sign of intelligence, is it, to embark on this course? If you get in a plane and have a look at the way this country works, you'll find that's not where the entitlements are.
Could you explain to us how this all works in this country at the moment?
Well, let's assume that someone in this country has a job and is discovered to be more or less completely incompetent.
OK, so he's on the board of a company, it's gone broke and two of the directors have syphoned off seven million dollars.
No, no. I'm talking about a person with an actual job. You've asked me about workers' entitlements. I'm talking about what happens on the floor shop.
Shop floor.
Shop floor, yes. I'm talking about what happens down there. There is a person who is clearly past it, who has become a bit of a menace, can't do the job.
Out the door.
Out the door. Gone.

What does his brother do?

No, I'm not talking about anyone in particular. I'm just explaining to you what happens when one of these tubs of lard has to be given the freckle.

What are his entitlements?

You see, that's exactly the sort of the-world-owes-me-a-living type of thinking I'm trying to eradicate. In my view, this harmless oaf has the world at his feet. He's got a trade...

Yes, he's probably got some experience.

Exactly. He's about sixty. Ideal time to start up a new career. Hot to trot, I would think, if he's got any brains. He's got his health.

Unless he hasn't, of course.

Unless he hasn't looked after himself, and he's become some sort of unidexter.

So, you think he should go on and try another job?

He's mad if he doesn't. What else is he going to do? He's got plenty of time.

What sort of job would he do?

Who cares what he does, for goodness' sake.

Mr Abbott, thanks for your time.

It actually looks funnier written down, doesn't it?

What does?

'Workers' entitlements.'

THE HON. JOHN HOWARD, PRIME MINISTER OF AUSTRALIA

In which the plan begins to bear fruit and unravel at the same time.

Mr Howard, thanks for your time.

Yes, very nice to be with you, thank you.

You must be very pleased with the polls that came out this week.

No. We don't care who they are. They're not coming out here. We've pulled the drawbridge up in this country. We made this announcement. We've had it, we've had it with them.

No, no, Mr Howard. The popularity poll. You're miles ahead.

Yes, I'm a little bit disinclined to put too much store by that sort of thing.

But you're in full election campaign mode now, aren't you?

We are, yes. We've decided when we're going to the people and it will be a short campaign but a terribly, terribly important one.

I'm sure. What do you think will happen?

It's very hard to say. And I would say to any of our people out there who may be vacillating, you mustn't take this for granted. I don't want people to get at all complacent about this. It's not going to be easy. It's going to be very close.

Close?

We've introduced, let's face it, some of the most radical reforms seen in the economic sector in this country in many years and I think people are often alarmed by change and they may opt for something more conservative.

More conservative than you are?

Yes. That's why we've got an opposition in this country.

Right. *(Bryan notices a mobile phone.)* **What is that?**

That's my phone.

Is it on?

Yes, of course it's on.

Mr Howard, it's customary when you're doing an interview to turn it off.

You will appreciate that, in the current international crisis, George

Bush may ring me at any time.

Yes, I appreciate that.

I need the phone with me at all times, so I'll just leave it there if you don't mind.

Can't he leave a message or something?

George Bush and I have a close personal relationship…

Sure, I understand that.

…particularly at this time of international instability. It is vital that I be able to take George Bush's call at any time.

OK, fine. I wonder if I could ask you about the effect of the GST on Australian business at the moment.

Yes—did you just hear a ringing sound? Was that a ringing sound?

No, I don't think so.

You didn't hear a ringing sound?

No.

'Ring ring', for example?

No. Mr Howard, small business has struggled with the GST, hasn't it? And we now have big business in all sorts of trouble—

You must have heard that slight digital buzzing then?

No. I didn't hear anything.

You don't think someone's trying to ring? I wouldn't want to miss the call.

No, I didn't hear anything. Mr Howard, consumer confidence is down. Coles Myer's retail figures…

That'll be him now. (*He picks up the phone.*) George? Yes, it's John Howard…Is anyone there?

No, there's nobody there.

I just saw this flickering light—I thought it must be a call.

No, that's the battery light.

Oh, the battery, oh.

Mr Howard, what are you doing about the asylum seekers?

I beg your pardon? Would you repeat the question?

What are you doing about the asylum seekers?

That is a very, very good question. Hold my phone for a minute, please.

Sorry?

This is a very, very important issue for this country. Very, very important. Australia has one of the most staggering, almost unique records in humanatropical matters.

Humanitarian.

Pardon?

Humanitarian.

Those too. Indeed. We have a very good record and we won't be held over a barrel just because the…

Refugees are desperate and we're a very large underpopulated country.

That's right. We're not going to be blackmailed in this country.

Now, Mr Howard, what do I do if this rings?

Oh, take a message. It'll only be George. This is a very, very important issue. We took a refugee into this country in 1984. The record will show that. I think we took another one in 1987.

Hang on, Mr Howard, I think it's the President.

(He picks up the phone.) George? Hello? There's nobody there.

Thanks for joining us.

THE HON. SIMON CREAN,
LEADER OF THE OPPOSITION

In which there is a problem with one of the starting gates.

Mr Crean, thanks for your time.
Thank you for inviting me in. It's good to be here.

How do you think you're going?
It's very hard to say. I wouldn't want to be overconfident, but I hope we're going well.

You're confident you're getting a message out there?
I certainly hope we're doing that. We've got some very good ads. Have you seen the one about John Howard not running the full term if he gets in?

Yes. Whose ad is that?
Whose ad is it? It's one of ours.

This is the one saying that Peter Costello will become PM?
That's right.

But which party is the ad for?
It's for our party. It's one of our ads.

But Mr Crean, aren't you trying to get rid of John Howard as the PM?
We certainly are. That's very much our idea, yes.

I thought so. You want people to vote for you in order to get rid of John Howard.
That's the theory.

Then why have you got an ad telling people that, if they vote Liberal, John Howard's not going to be the PM anymore?
I think you may have misunderstood our ad.

Did you pay any money for the ad?
I can check that for you.

Mr Crean, the Liberal Party policies and the Labor Party policies are awfully similar.
Haven't we got some good policies? We've got some crackers this time.

Yes, but they're the same as the government's. I mean, what's the difference?

There are significant differences.

What are they? Give us an example. Different in what area?

I'm thinking.

Your policy on the asylum seekers, for example.

That's the same as the government's, by all means.

Your policy on the war—it's the same as the government's.

That's the same as the government's, yes. But what about areas where our policies are not the same as the government's? Let's talk about those.

Certainly. Like what?

Like health.

Same as the government's.

No it's not.

What's the difference?

On health?

Yes.

The government's got the same policy we've got.

Yes, but they're both the same. What about the environment?

We certainly don't have the same policy the government's got on the environment.

What's the difference, Mr Crean?

The government's got the same policy we've got on the environment.

Mr Crean, it's the same policy, that's my point.

I'm trying to explain the difference to you. You've asked me—

OK, what is the difference?

Well, the policy isn't the area in which the difference lies. There's obviously a difference between our having the same policy as the government and the government having the same policy we've got.

But are they the same policy?

No. There is a huge difference. For example, in education, we in the Labor Party believe that we should provide the very highest quality of education we possibly can in this country.

This is 'Knowledge Nation'?

No, this is Ignoralia at the moment. We'd like it to become Knowledge Nation.

You'd like us to become a smarter country?

I don't think we can afford not to be a smarter country.

In that case, why have you got the same policies as the government of Ignoralia on all these other issues?

Have you actually seen a copy of the government's policy document?

Yes, I have.

Have you seen a copy of our policy document?

Yes, I have.

Yes, and you can tell which is which. How do you tell?

Yours has got a yellow cover.

I rest my case. There's not much I can do for you, is there? I mean, you've answered your own question.

The policies are the same, Mr Crean.

No, I think I've answered your question. Have you got any others?

Mr Crean, thanks for your time.

Nothing else?

THE HON. JOHN HOWARD, PRIME MINISTER OF AUSTRALIA

In which victory is snatched from the jaws of the open sea.

Mr Howard, thanks for your time.

Thank you very much and good evening.

First of all, congratulations.

Thank you very much indeed.

That was quite a win.

It was a fantastic win. I'm very happy with the win. I think I'm right in saying, and correct me if I'm wrong, that would be one of the greatest victories in Australian political history.

Did you think you'd win?

We had some indications but of course there are various factors operating in different parts of the country, so it was difficult to know.

And yet in the event it was very emphatic. Mr Howard, what are you going to do now?

Do you just want to mention the Menzies thing?

I'm terribly sorry. Mr Howard, you're now the most successful Liberal leader since Sir Robert Menzies.

Yes indeed, I certainly am. *(Mutters)* Do you also want to mention the Fraser reference while we're here?

Sorry, and you've really stuck it up Malcolm Fraser, haven't you?

No, no, no, I only meant to refer to the fact that, similarly, I have now got in for a third term…

Oh right. Well done, indeed. Mr Howard, what are you going to do now?

…as did Malcolm Fraser, the famously long-serving Liberal leader of recent times.

Yes, and what about the future?

And Bob Hawke, the long-serving Labor leader who now has also been completely eclipsed by me.

Yes, so Mr Howard, what are you going to do now?

It's a great honour too. Can I just say, this is a wonderful country. It's a great honour which has been entrusted to me by the Australian public, and here I don't refer only to the 51 per cent who voted for One Nation…

For the Coalition.

I beg your pardon?

For the Coalition.

For the Coalition. But also the 49 per cent of disaffected elitists who refused to toe the line. You're always going to get these people. You're not going to make everyone happy. That's the nature of democracy.

Mr Howard, how are you now going to bring this country together again?

What do you mean, 'bring the country together again'?

Well, it's been a very divisive time, hasn't it?

It certainly has. Yes, indeed.

In fact, the last few months have been…

Oh yes, oh yes. Oh yes. It's been fantastic!

What about the succession, Mr Howard? Are you now going to hand over…

Hang on a minute. Why are you asking me about the succession?

…to Peter Costello.

Sorry? Why are you asking me this question?

There has been some speculation about the…

Did Peter Costello ask you to ask me this?

No, not at all.

Are you sure Peter Costello…

I just wondered. It's an obvious question, isn't it?

Are you from Melbourne?

No, why would I be from Melbourne?

I think we're finished with this subject. Come on, you're being divisive. I'm the PM. Have you been enjoying the cricket? The cricket's good, isn't it?

Are you going to retire, Mr Howard?

Not immediately, no. Ultimately, I'll retire. Menzies retired.

Sure.

Fraser unfortunately didn't have the brains. Neither did Hawke.

Right. Thanks for your time.

No, no, no. I'm still here. I'll decide when we're finished.

OK. Well, thanks for your time, Mr Howard.

I'm telling you, I'll decide when we're finished. Shut up and sign your piece of paper.

PART III
THE FINAL PUSH
2001–2003

THE HON. PETER COSTELLO, TREASURER OF AUSTRALIA

In which the cost of victory is expressed in terms everyone can understand.

Mr Costello, thanks for your time.
Good evening, it's very nice of you to invite me on the program.
Mr Costello, are you happy with the new Cabinet?
Absolutely. A very good Cabinet, some very good people in there.
Some exciting, fresh new ideas?
Are you still talking about the Cabinet?
Yes. Are you pleased with the economic position?
Australia's economic outlook is very strong. Very strong indeed.
That's good.
It is good. It means we can get on and rebuild the surplus.
I was going to ask you about that. What happened to the surplus?
Didn't we have a huge surplus at one time?
We did, Australia's economic management in recent years has really
been…
Pretty spectacular.
…something of a triumph, yes.
So where's the surplus?
Well, we had one or two expenses. I mean, we've had a refugee crisis
to…
Generate.
…deal with. And that was a very, very…
Cheap trick.
…expensive exercise and, of course, we've also undertaken a lot of
new programs in the light of…
The need to get re-elected.
…the need of the broader community.
Mr Costello, why aren't we still under threat from the asylum seekers?
I'm sorry. Are we not?
We don't seem to be. It's not in the paper these days.

Oh really? I must get out more.

I thought they were coming down here in their thousands.

That was certainly my impression.

So where are they now?

Well, I gather from what you seem to be saying that since the federal election the asylum seekers have found us a lot less attractive as a destination.

Or maybe it's not in the papers as often?

Yes, although why that would be, I don't know, do you?

Maybe they've stopped throwing their children overboard.

Hang on. I don't know if we actually knew they were throwing their children overboard exactly.

No, but we were told that they were.

We were told that it had been reported, that there was a possibility that in certain instances it may have been a possible construction, that elements of overboard-throwing had occurred in some specified nautical areas at that time.

We were told that by the Minister of Defence, weren't we?

He didn't say it had happened. He said it had been reported that it had happened.

Yes, but in what capacity did he say it had been reported that it had happened?

In his capacity as the defence minister.

A most reliable authority.

It was Peter Reith.

Yes, but even so.

We're getting out of my area slightly. Can I just say that I can't answer questions about directly what happened up there. I wasn't there. I was actually very, very busy here.

Doing what?

Trying to work out how to pay for it, young man.

Mr Costello, thank you for your time.

Don't thank me, son. Wait until you see what it cost.

THE HON. DARYL WILLIAMS, ATTORNEY-GENERAL OF AUSTRALIA

In which the cost of victory is further explained in terms everyone can see don't work.

Daryl Williams, thanks for your time.
It's very good to be here, thank you.
Attorney-General, we're having a lot of problems up in Woomera at the moment, aren't we?
We have been experiencing one or two problems in the Woomera area recently, yes. The people being held in detention there are engaging in what I would describe as acts of destruction.
Wanton destruction.
'Acts of wanton destruction', yes.
Why are the people being held there?
These are people who are waiting for their applications for refugee status to be processed.
And why don't they like being in a jail in Woomera?
I've got no idea.
Is it a nice place?
It's a beautiful place, an absolutely beautiful place. It's got walls.
A roof?
Roof, yes.
Fence?
A beautiful fence. It's got one of the best fences I think I've ever seen in my life.
Really? Any trees?
No trees. But a fantastic fence.
Flowers?
Flowers, no. The fence is a ripper, but there aren't any flowers.
Just walls and roof and the fence?
Yes, an absolutely beautiful fence.
Is it near anything?

The building?

Yes.

Yes. It's very near the fence.

I mean, are there towns nearby?

No, this is a detention centre. It's not a hotel we're talking about.

Is there a visiting area?

What's a visiting area?

You know, a place for people to visit people.

No, nobody's going to be visiting these people. It's in Woomera.

And what do these people want?

They want to have their applications processed and get out.

And become part of the community?

That's right. But they're not going to do that so long as they behave in
the way in which they have been. They set fire to the place. We're not
going to be intimida—

**What would happen if they stop causing problems at the detention
centre?**

What they've got to understand is that they must stop these acts of
wanton destruction. They've got to cease being vandals and settle
down.

And what will happen if they do?

If they do, we can then look at the possibility of perhaps engaging in
some discussion that might ultimately move towards an application
review of some kind, at some stage, in respect of some of these people.
And actual processing may result in some instances.

**But Minister, isn't that the problem? Isn't that the reason for their
actions? That we're not processing their applications?**

We're not going to process anything at all under any circumstances, if
they keep behaving in the way in which they have been.

**Aren't they behaving like that purely because you're not doing these
applications for them?**

We will refuse to process anything so long as people are acting like
this. That's what they've got to understand and that's what I'm
indicating to you.

OK. And what happens if they do stop?
If they don't stop, we're not going to process anything. That's the
position.
And if they *do* stop?
Unless they stop, nothing will happen.
So we'll hear their applications if they *do* stop?
We won't be hearing anything unless they stop. That's what I'm saying
to you.
Yes, but if they stop, will we process their applications for them?
Let me put this another way. The way to get us to hear their
applications is to stop doing what they've been doing. They've got to
stop behaving like vandals.
They've got to stop engaging in acts of wanton destruction?
Wanton destruction, yes. Your term. They've got to stop doing that.
**But if they stop the acts of wanton destruction, will we process their
applications?**
Not if they keep behaving the way they have been.
Daryl Williams, thank you very much.
Thank you. I just wanted to clarify the government's position.

THE HON. PHILIP RUDDOCK, MINISTER FOR IMMIGRATION AND MULTICULTURAL AND INDIGENOUS AFFAIRS

In which the cost of the victory is yet further explained, this time by a professional.

Mr Ruddock, thanks for your time.

I simply make the point that I'm here, I've made myself available and these things can now proceed in accordance with the way they're done.

Thanks for coming in.

I simply make the point that I've made myself available.

And I'm delighted you're here, Mr Ruddock, and thanks for your time.

I simply make the point that a lot of Australians might think this behaviour of yours is not appropriate.

What, thanking you?

Yes.

That's just a courtesy.

I simply make the point that why establish a precedent if you don't need to?

I'm only thanking you, Mr Ruddock. It's not a very dangerous precedent, is it?

I simply make the point, why establish a precedent?

What are you suggesting I say? Nothing?

I simply make the point.

OK, Mr Ruddock, are you happy with the way Australia is handling its immigration at the moment?

We're going very well.

We've got people rioting in detention centres, people sewing up their lips...

I simply make the point that what we're trying to do with these people...

They must be pretty desperate to want to sew their lips together.

…I simply make the point that what we're trying to do with these people is to process them as quickly as possible and determine which are legitimate refugees and which are not.

Mr Ruddock, the asylum-seeker crisis seems to be getting worse not better, doesn't it?

Getting worse for whom?

For the asylum seekers.

I simply make the point that we're trying to get this processed as fast as possible and to make a determination about whether those asylum seekers are legitimate refugees.

What is an *illegitimate* refugee?

An illegitimate refugee is a refugee who is not a legitimate refugee.

Why would anyone pretend to be a refugee?

In order to get into Australia.

They would take a perilous sea voyage across the ocean and end up in a detention centre, sew their lips together out in a hot desert in the middle of South Australia.

I simply make the point that what we're trying to do is process those refugees as fast as possible and to make a determination about which are legitimate and which are not.

And to determine who might come into Australia.

Yes, if their behaviour is appropriate.

Is there a Department of Appropriate Behaviour?

I will make a determination about what is appropriate and what is not.

Why can't we process them faster?

I simply make the point we're processing them as fast as we can.

Why is it that everyone who went to New Zealand has been processed already?

I simply make the point that we're trying to process the ones in Australia as fast as we can.

Why have they been able to process those refugees over in New Zealand and yet we haven't been able to?

I simply make the point that we're trying to process them as fast as possible.

Mr Ruddock, thank you for coming in.

I simply repeat the point that I don't think your behaviour is appropriate.

In thanking you for coming in?

Yes.

I thought you said there wasn't a department of appropriate behaviour.

There isn't.

In which case I might be the best judge of my own behaviour, thanks.

I simply make the point that I don't think your behaviour is appropriate.

Thank you, Mr Ruddock.

I simply make the point your courtesy isn't appropriate.

Thank you for coming in, Mr Ruddock.

Stop being reasonable, Bryan. It's unAustralian.

Thank you very much.

Stop it.

THE HON. JOHN HOWARD, PRIME MINISTER OF AUSTRALIA

In which the cost of the victory becomes increasingly obvious.

Mr Howard, thanks for your time.
It's very good to be with you. Thank you for inviting me in.
I wonder if I could ask you about the babies overboard business?
Yes. Certainly. The story that's coming out now or the story we told at the time?
The story that we're getting now.
This week's story?
Yes.
The Monday story? The Tuesday story? Or the one that's broken subsequently?
Well, perhaps today's story.
Today's story?
Yes.
This morning's story or the one we're using now?
What's the difference?
The point I'm making is I have no intention of discussing the period when Peter Reith was saying one thing and I was saying another.
Neither do I. That's fine.
Look, please don't interrupt. I'm trying to answer your question with honesty and integrity…
Both of them?
Simultaneously, yes. And you're interrupting. That's not very helpful.
OK, I'm sorry.
Neither have I any intention of discussing the period when Peter remembered that he was told it wasn't true but he'd forgotten to tell me.
Why would he have neglected to do that?
Don't interrupt, please. It's not helpful at all.
OK, I'm sorry. Go ahead.

Then of course we had the period when Peter thought he may have told me that the thing was completely untrue but he didn't tell me in English.

Oh, that's right. I remember that. Yes, yes, yes. How long did that version last?

It didn't last very long.

It was almost subliminal, wasn't it?

I don't think that was one of our better ones. Then we stumbled on what I believe is an absolute cracker, which was that we were all grossly misinformed by an incompetent public servant.

Public servant. That's the current version, isn't it?

What's the time?

7.55.

Yes, that's still current, I don't think we've found any involvement that Peter Hollingworth may have with this issue as yet.

So what does he do now, Peter Reith?

Since he retired from parliament? Peter was lucky enough to secure employment negotiating government defence contracts. *(Laughs.)*

(Laughs.) **Really?**

Yes. *(Laughs.)* I'm sorry. I'll try that again, sorry. Just ask me that again.

So what does he do now, Peter Reith?

Since he retired from parliament, Peter has been lucky enough to get a job negotiating government defence contracts. *(Both parties doubled-over laughing, desperately trying to compose themselves.)*

Sorry, that is very funny.

I'm sorry. I apologise.

Can I do it again? So what does Peter Reith do now?

Since he retired from politics, Peter... *(fighting back laughter)*...I'm sorry. It took us four hours to get this right in the Cabinet room before we could even...

OK. You look that way and I'll look this way. *(They face different directions.)*

Yes. Now ask me again.

So what does Peter Reith do now?
Peter Reith, at the moment, is…*(Explodes with laughter.)*
Maybe we'll move on. Let me ask you another question. Why do you think people would throw their own children into the sea?
Why would anyone believe that parents would throw their children in the sea? That's too hard. Ask me the Peter Reith one again.
OK, all right. So, Prime Minister, what does Peter Reith do now?
Peter Reith has got a job selling government defence contracts.
(Both parties erupt into laughter.)

THE HON. GARETH EVANS, CHERYL KERNOT AND MR LAURIE OAKES

In which we are joined by some old pantomime favourites.

OK. Buzzers working?
Gareth Evans? *(Gareth Evans' buzzer buzzes.)*
Cheryl Kernot? *(Cheryl Kernot's buzzer gongs.)* **Laurie Oakes?** *(Laurie Oakes' buzzer screeches—like a jet engine.)* **Terrific. OK, first question.**
(Gareth Evans' buzzer.) **No, hang on, Gareth. Hang on, Gareth. What is wrong with this statement…**
(Gareth Evans' buzzer.) **No, Gareth, hang on. You're a bit ahead of yourself there…'All cats are dogs'?**
(Gareth Evans' buzzer.)
Gareth?
That should be, 'Some cats are dogs'.
No, sorry.
(Cheryl Kernot's buzzer.)
Cheryl?
Um, 'All dogs are cats?'
No.
(Laurie Oakes' buzzer.)
Laurie?
'All cats are arseholes?'
No, I'm afraid not, Laurie. Look, I think we'll move on to the next question. What is logic?
(Gareth Evans' buzzer.)
Gareth?
Everyone knows what logic is, Bryan.
Well, what is it Gareth? That was the question.
I can think of plenty of examples of it.
(Laurie Oakes' buzzer.)
Laurie?
What was the question? You want to know what logic actually is?

That's right, Laurie.

(Cheryl Kernot's buzzer.) Yes. Cheryl?

Yes, lots of examples of logic spring to mind, don't they?

Give me an example, Cheryl Kernot.

All right. Well, if I tell you everything...

What do you mean 'everything', Cheryl?

I mean absolutely everything.

What about?

About everything. If I tell you absolutely everything about everything...

Yes, but what sort of things, Cheryl?

Well, Laurie's a turd, for example.

(Laurie Oakes' buzzer.)

OK, hang on, Laurie, hang on, Laurie, steady. Go on, Cheryl. If you tell me everything, what?

If I tell you everything, I don't have to tell you everything.

No, that's not right.

(Laurie Oakes' buzzer.)

Laurie, an example of logic?

Yes. I know everything about who's having an affair in the public life of Australia, and it's my duty as a genius to tell the public, and I can only think of *one*.

One affair? No-one else in public life in Australia is having an affair, Laurie?

Oh, whoops, that's wrong, isn't it?

I'm afraid that's not right at all, Laurie.

(Gareth Evans' buzzer.)

Gareth?

The reason I denied I was having an extramarital affair was to save my marriage.

No, you're guessing, aren't you? *(New character arrives.)* Yes?

Do you want someone to read out the scores?

No. There aren't any scores. Nobody's got anything right yet.

I know that, but do you want somebody to read that out?

No, not really. Who are you?

I'm Michael Wooldridge. If you've got any jobs that need doing, give us a whistle.

Haven't you got anything better to do?

No, not anymore.

Why not?

(All three buzzers sound forever.)

A SENIOR BANKING EXECUTIVE

In which the country continues to move like a well-oiled machine.

Thanks for your time.

Take a number, will you? I'll be with you in a minute.

You're one of Australia's leading bankers.

Yes. Just take a number, son. I'll be with you as soon as I possibly can.

How many banks do we have in Australia?

There are three or four of us operating in what is technically described as the banking sector. We're all in—what's that thing called?

Sydney.

No, no. It's in the paper all the time.

Russell Crowe?

No. It's where there are only a few of you and you're pretending there are quite a lot of you and you actually control everything.

Competition?

Competition! We're all in competition with one another.

So why have you closed my branch?

Is this an inquiry?

Yes.

Inquiries down the end there, son.

Well, is there anyone else I can speak to?

Someone else in the bank?

Yes.

No.

Why not?

He's at lunch. Do take a number. I'll get to you as soon as I finish doing this.

But hang on, who am I supposed to talk to?

Is this an inquiry?

Yes.

Inquiries down the end there, son.

It would be a lot easier, actually, if you could just answer my question.

Are you on the internet?

No, I'm not.

What you do is you go on the internet and you go to our website…

But I'm not on the internet.

You've got to be on the internet to go to our website.

But I don't want to go to your website.

You can't do your internet banking without going on the internet. You need to go to our website.

Look, excuse me, I don't want to do my banking on the internet. I want to go and do my banking at a branch.

Yes, well just take a number, son and go down there. I'll be with you as soon as I possibly can.

There's no-one down there.

No-one down at inquiries?

No.

But there will be when you go down there.

No, I mean there's no-one working down there.

That's right. We're a bank, son. We're not here to provide light entertainment. How are we going to make a quid out of answering a lot of silly questions?

Listen, I can't do my banking because you shut my branch and I want to know why.

You want to know why we shut your branch?

Yes.

That's an inquiry. Take it down to inquiries.

Where am I supposed to do my banking?

Are you on the internet?

Is this an inquiry?

Of course it's an inquiry. I'm trying to find out if…

Inquiries down the end there.

There's no-one there. I'm trying to help you, son. You want to know how to do your banking?

Is this an inquiry?

Of course it's a bloody inquiry.

Inquiries down the end there.

I give up.

Yes, I worked that out. My question is where do I do my banking?

I'm sorry, I'm afraid all our usual methods of avoiding the issue are currently engaged. Your call has been placed in the toilet.

THE HON. JOHN HOWARD, PETER COSTELLO AND SIMON CREAN

In which a clash of the Titans is arranged, and most edifying it proves to be.

Right. Buzzers working. John Howard?

Buzz.

Peter Costello?

Buzz.

Simon Crean?

Buzz.

Right. OK. If you were letting the market run the economy and the market fell over, what would you do?

(No-one answers.)

Are those buzzers working? John Howard?

Buzz.

Peter Costello?

Buzz.

Simon Crean?

Buzz.

We'll go on to the next one. If you deregulated the financial markets and took away all the rules, what rules would then govern the behaviour of the financial markets? *(No-one answers. Bryan talks to the director.)* **Shane we've got a problem here. Are these buzzers working?**
Yes.
Are those buzzers working? John Howard?

Buzz.

Peter Costello?

Buzz.

Simon Crean?

Buzz.

We'll try another one. If you went into business to make a huge amount of money, and you had to give your shareholders anything that was left over, why would there be anything left over? John

Howard, you must know the answer to this.

Can I phone a friend?

Yes, let's phone a friend. We're dialling the number now. Hello?

(Peter Costello answers.) Hello?

No, John, you can't call Peter. (Turns to next question.) Here's one you'll all get. What is superannuation?

Buzz.

John Howard?

Smaller?

Buzz.

Peter Costello?

It used to be an amount of money you put aside for when you retired.

Good, but I want to know what it is now.

Buzz.

Simon Crean?

Is it something to do with the 60/40 Rule?

No, Simon. Final question. General question. What is humanity?

Buzz.

John Howard?

The guy who runs Western Mining?

No, that's Hugh Morgan.

Buzz.

Peter Costello?

Is it something to do with Philip Ruddock?

No, I'm afraid it's not.

Buzz.

Simon Crean?

Is it when there's no Opposition?

No, that's Australia. (A new person enters.) Hello? Who are you?

I'm Ray Williams.

And what's your problem Ray?

Buzzzzzzzzzzz.

(All buzzers buzz forever.)

THE HON. RON BOSWELL, PARLIAMENTARY SECRETARY TO THE MINISTER FOR TRANSPORT AND REGIONAL SERVICES

In which…working?…of a great national asset is…hello?…buggered.

Senator Boswell, thanks for your time.
(Off.) I don't know where they are. I can't see him. Am I supposed to be able to see him?
Senator Boswell, can you hear me?
(Off.) Shouldn't I be able to see him?
Can you hear me, Senator Boswell?
(Off.) If I'm going to be interviewed by him, surely I should be seeing him.
Senator Boswell, can you hear me?
(Off.) I'm supposed to be here at this time, aren't I?
Senator Boswell?
(Off.) Yes, well tell them I can't see him.
Senator Boswell?
Oh, there he is. Hello, hello.
Yes, Senator Boswell. How are you?
Bryan?
Yes.
How are you?
Good thanks. How are you?
Good, terrific. Good on you.
Thanks for your time.
It's a pleasure.
You said this week that you were satisfied with the standard of communications in Australia and that it had improved.
(Off.) I know he's asking me a question. I can see his lips moving.
Senator Boswell, can you hear me?

(Off.) I can't hear the question. Can you hear me?

I can't hear him at all.

(Off.) Are they aware that I can't hear him? If he can't hear me, I'll ring him.

Look, I'll give him a call. *(Into phone.)* **Could I have the number for Senator Boswell, please.**

(Into phone.) Hello, can you get me a number, please, for Bryan Dawe.

(Into phone.) **He's in the country somewhere.**

(Into phone.) Dawe with a 'D'.

(Into phone.) **No, no, not the Senator Motel. Boswell. Senator Boswell.**

(Into phone.) He hasn't got anything to do with windscreens—windscreens? What on earth have I said that would give you that—no, he's a journalist.

(Into phone.) **No, B-O-S-W-E-L-L.**

(Into phone.) Dawe with a 'D'.

(The picture comes back.) **Hello. Senator Boswell? Oh, there he is now.**

Is that you, Bryan?

Yes.

G'day, how are you?

Good, terrific. Can you hear me now OK?

I can hear you now perfectly, Bryan, yes.

What is your telephone number, in case that happens again?

I was trying to ring you actually. My number?

Yes.

My number is…*(picture disappears)*

Senator Boswell?

(Off.) I can't hear him at all.

(Off.) **Where has he gone?**

What's happened? I can't hear him. Oh, hang on, I can see him now, but I can't hear him.

He's back, he's back. Are we having a—Hello?

Hello, Bryan.

Hi. How are you?

Sorry about that.

Sorry, we're just having some problems with the line.

Yes, I was just organising Telstra to have a look at what the problem is.
I've spoken to them, and they're going to look into it.

When?

Tuesday between 2 and 7.

OK. We'll just have to carry on the best way we can.

Yes, we'll do the best we can.

So you said you're happy with the standard of communication in Australia?

Yes, I did, Bryan.

Particularly the rural and regional areas of Australia?

(Cut to a different person at a conference speaking Japanese.)

And so you think that the sale of Telstra should go ahead?

(Distorted voice speaks at high speed.) I do, yes. I think things…*(distorted speaks at slow speed)*…have improved a great deal.

Terrific. Senator Boswell, thanks for your time. Senator Boswell?

(Off.) Where's he gone now? I mean, this is ridiculous. I'm in the right place. I'm supposed to be here. *(He dials a number.)* Hello? Can you get me another number? No, look, you won't cock this one up. It begins with 'Z'.

A SENIOR EXECUTIVE AT HIH INSURANCE LIMITED

In which an oxygen mask drops down from the compartment above our seat.

Thanks very much for your time.

Pleasure.

You were in a significant executive position at HIH.

Yes. I was.

Have you given evidence yet?

Yes, I'm in there now. Is this what you want to ask about, is it?

Yes.

You want to ask about management at HIH?

Yes.

How the place worked and so on?

Yes.

Can I make a suggestion?

Yes.

You give me a million dollars…

A million dollars? Why would I give you a million dollars?

Well, you want me to come in here and do this work with you.

Yes, but it's only an interview.

But it's an important one. You can't just go out and get anyone to do it.

I want to interview someone who was intimately involved in the running of HIH.

I'm glad we understand each other.

So what do we do?

You give me a million dollars.

What's the million dollars for?

It's an inducement.

An inducement for what?

An inducement for me to do the interview. You've got to induce me to do it.

But you've agreed to do it.

Well, call it an agreement fee. I don't give a toss what we call it. Just give me a million dollars.

If I give you a million dollars you won't *need* to do the interview.

No, but I'll do it anyway.

Why?

Because I think we're on to something. You give me a million dollars. I'll give you a million dollars to start.

We haven't *got* a million dollars.

Not a problem.

Seems like a pretty big problem to me.

No, we'll get the money when we sell shares in the interview.

Why would we sell shares in the interview?

Our options aren't going to be worth much if we don't convert into stock.

What options?

Part of our pay for doing this is an options package.

But it's an interview.

Correction. It's an 'entertainment opportunity'.

But someone's going to have to buy it for all this to work.

No. Someone's only got to buy the *idea* that someone will buy it.

Who's going to buy the idea that someone will buy an interview?

The guy who's selling the idea that someone will buy the idea will have to believe that or he won't be able to sell it.

But who's the end-user? Someone must ultimately be paying for the whole set-up.

Don't worry about it. The taxpayer will pick up any losses.

The taxpayer doesn't even know we're having this conversation.

No, but anyone who does their dough here will write it off against their tax.

But the taxpayer didn't cause it.

No. The taxpayer's not a very entrepreneurial character.

Just pays tax.

Good example. He's an absolute idiot.

THE HON. RICHARD ALSTON, MINISTER FOR COMMUNICATIONS, INFORMATION TECHNOLOGY AND THE ARTS

In which we once again see that the relationship between the poacher and the gamekeeper is subject to some confusion.

Senator Alston, thanks for your time.

You're fired.

Thank you, Senator Alston. What's your reaction to the criticism at the moment of the administration of the ABC?

Criticism from whom?

From people who don't agree with the cost cutting and the drift towards privatisation.

Let me say something that will make the position very, very clear. The administration of the ABC is the responsibility of those people who are charged with that responsibility. Without wanting to surprise you, it has occurred to us that the success of the ABC has not been completely unalloyed in recent times. And we want to improve that. We want to improve that performance.

And there will be people who resist that change?

There are always people opposed to progress and we will expect some resistance to that change.

Senator Alston, why did you put a person who's worked in the public broadcasting arena for twenty years on the board of the Stock Exchange?

No, you've lost me there, I'm afraid. What have I done?

You've appointed a person who's been involved in public broadcasting for twenty years...

Yes. Involved in public broadcasting for twenty years...

...to the board of the Stock Exchange.

I've put him on the board of the Stock Exchange? Why would I do that?

That was my question, Senator Alston.

I wouldn't do it, would I? I mean, what would he know? He wouldn't be able to do the job…think about your question. What would a person who has spent the bulk of his working life in public broadcasting know about the equities market?

That's what I would have thought.

It's a completely irrational, idiotic suggestion. He wouldn't know how to do the job. I wouldn't do a thing like that. I'd check your facts, if I were you.

I do beg your pardon, Senator Alston. I see what I've done here.

You're fired.

I see the mistake. I'm sorry.

That's right, you should apologise. What you're suggesting I have done is completely irrational, very stupid and entirely self-contradictory.

My notes are wrong, I do apologise. They're quite wrong. What you did was put the head of the Stock Exchange on the board of the national broadcaster. I really am sorry.

That's right. That's completely different.

I do apologise.

You should apologise. You're fired.

Thank you. Senator, is it also true that you are introducing a new system to assess the political bias of the ABC. Is that correct?

Now that is correct. We're introducing what I would describe as 'a new system of review'.

Why do you need to do that?

In order to ensure the right to free speech, we first need to determine who has that right.

Shouldn't everyone have it?

You think everyone in the whole country should have the right to free speech?

I suppose my question is how can something be a 'right' if not everyone has it?

Yes. What's your name?

Bryan Dawe.

Ever been in trouble with the police before for any reason at all, Bryan?

No.

What we're trying to do here, Bryan, is to organise a new system, a process of review for the ABC. The ABC is a very important organisation. It's a very large organisation…

Yes, I appreciate all that.

It broadcasts right across the country, Bryan, and it costs a great deal of money to run.

Yes. Are the commercial channels biased would you say, Minister?

No, the commercial channels are not biased, Bryan. They're very conservative. We don't have a problem with them.

How can they not be biased if you're saying they're very conservative?

Bryan, the commercial channels are not the issue. We don't have a problem with them. They are not the problem.

You don't think this could be construed as an attempt to censor the national broadcaster at all?

Absolutely no attempt here to censor the ABC.

Wouldn't people on the ABC…

Voiceover: The views expressed in this program are not those of ABC management.

Minister. You're on the ABC now. Are you being biased?

No, I'm not being biased. I'm opposed to bias at the ABC.

So am I, Minister, but I'm talking to you.

The ABC has absolutely nothing to fear if it just watches how it goes politically.

Yes, but surely the ABC's job is to provide a service to all the community, Minister, not just the government?

The ABC's job, since you bring it up Bryan, is to provide adequate shipping times and reliable grain prices and quite a lot of Mantovani music, and the sooner they get on with that the sooner this problem of bias will go away.

What sort of result are you looking for from the ABC?

What is the government looking for by way of a result from the national broadcaster? Is that your question?

Yes.

We'd take half a billion…Prior to auction.

Minister, won't the ABC then fail in its obligation to… *(Music by Enya drowns out interviewer.)* **Am I fired?**

You're fired.

Thank you.

THE HON. DAVID KEMP, MINISTER FOR THE ENVIRONMENT

In which we see, once again, Australia achieving prominence at the highest level internationally.

Dr Kemp, thanks for your time.
Good evening. Very nice to be talking to you.
How's it going over there at the environmental summit in Johannesburg?
Well, it's a very, very interesting experience for me. It's a most fascinating place.
How did your address go?
I've got to say it was a bit character-building. But, if nothing else, I think that I've certainly expressed some very interesting ideas.
Did anyone come up to you and say that you'd expressed some interesting ideas?
I haven't had a lot of contact with the other delegates since I formally stated Australia's position.
Yes, but as Minister for the Environment, surely you must have met other environment ministers.
I beg your pardon? As Minister for the Environment?
Yes, you are the Minister for the Environment, aren't you?
Just bear with me, will you. (*He dials a number on his mobile phone.*) Minister *for* the Environment, Minister *for the Environment*, you said?
Minister for the Environment, yes.
Minister *for the Environment*?
Yes.
Yes. That's what I thought you said. (*Speaks into mobile phone.*) John? Yes, it's David…
Isn't that why you're over there? Doing the address?
(*into phone still*)…I'm just doing an interview with somebody at the moment, John…No, with somebody back there. Sorry, what's your name?

Bryan Dawe.

…with Bryan Doyle.

No, Bryan Dawe.

…and he's telling me, John, that I'm the Minister *for* the Environment. Is that right?

Well, it must be right, Minister. That's why you're at the summit.

…Look, John, I've got to tell you, I wish you'd pointed that out a little bit earlier. Well, because I'm over here arguing the opposite.

Minister, you are the Minister for the Environment.

…John, I'm actually over here saying the Kyoto protocols aren't the point.

Of course they're the point. How can you move forward, Minister, if you don't accept the protocols?

…You know what I said, John, because you saw it and because I discussed it with you before leaving. I basically got up here and told them all to go and get stuffed.

Minister? Dr Kemp?

I don't care how good it looked, John. It's completely out of keeping with our international thinking on the environment, which, it turns out, is what the conference is about.

Minister, does John know that Russia and China have agreed to sign the protocols?

Hang on a minute, Barry, I'm talking to John.

And the fact that Australia is at the moment in the grip of the worst drought it's had in its history?

That's a very good point. Good point. Bill makes a good point, John.

Bryan.

…A lot of the people at the conference are saying to me how can I, coming as I do from a country with a history of drought and which is currently in the grip of one of the worst droughts in its own history, come here and argue that we shouldn't do anything about it?

Dr Kemp, I wonder if…

…All right, I'll give it a go.

Dr Kemp?

…Of course it's a long shot but I'll try anything at this stage, John.

Dr Kemp?

…Go and have a look at your telly, John. I'll give it a crack. *(Hangs up.)*

Dr Kemp? Dr Kemp, as Minister for the Environment…

Can I just correct you there?

Yes, what?

I'm not the Australian Minister for the Environment.

What do you mean you're not? What are you?

I'm actually a wildebeest who has roamed unaccountably from his reservation and finds himself in a television studio trying to conduct an interview about the environment with an interviewer in another country.

Dr Kemp, thanks for your time.

Put yourself in my position.

THE HON. PHILIP RUDDOCK, MINISTER FOR IMMIGRATION AND MULTICULTURAL AND INDIGENOUS AFFAIRS

In which the interminable is also clarified.

Mr Ruddock, thanks for your time.
Pleasure.
This business of Australia excising parts of itself.
Yes, temporarily.
Oh, it's going to unexcise them is it?
Yes, those areas will be re-conquered later.
Why was it done in secret?
It wasn't done in secret.
It wasn't done in the parliament though, was it?
Not telling.
Who was there?
We were both there.
Who were both of you?
Not telling.
Why?
It's just not something we want to talk about.
It's a secret, isn't it?
No, it's not.
Why have we done it? Why are we cutting bits of our own country away? These islands off the coast are part of Australia.
We have done it in order to protect Australia from being invaded by asylum seekers who will then be able to claim the privileges due to them under Australian law.
We don't want that?
No, that happened once before and it was an absolute disaster.
When was that?
When the white man got here. Just over two hundred years ago

exactly the same thing happened.

Oh that's right. You're the Minister for Aboriginal Affairs aren't you?

I am. And the Aborigines were living here when boats started arriving.

And did they excise parts of their country?

Well, that was a bit different. In that case the country belonged to the people who were arriving in the boats.

And they excised the Aborigines?

Yes.

The boot was on the other foot?

The position was different, yes.

So if we see them heading for a bit of Australia we define that bit as not being part of Australia?

That's right.

How do you do that? What's the procedure?

If we see someone heading for Australia...

In a boat?

Yes, this doesn't apply to people in planes. If we see a boat coming, I duck down the corridor and have a quick meeting with the Minister for Semantics and...

The Minister for Semantics?

Yes.

Who is the Minister for Semantics?

As it happens?

Yes.

I am.

Why don't you excise the big main island? It's a much bigger target.

And just let them try to hit a couple of little outlying bits?

Yes.

Because the people who are running the country are in the big bit.

Who are they?

Not telling.

THE HON. JOHN HOWARD, PRIME MINISTER OF AUSTRALIA

In which we hear some wonderful fables from Aesop, among others.

Mr Howard, thanks for your time.
Pleasure.
This last year has brought about a huge change in the way Australians regard regional security, hasn't it?
It has. There's been a loss of innocence.
Yes, when did this happen? Could you date this for us?
I think it began just before the last election.
Going back, take us over what you've said.
I've tried to best represent the interests and concerns of the Australian public.
But take us back to when all this started. Australians were all living happily here…
Yes.
Minding their own business…
Yes.
And so what did you do?
I yelled out that there was a wolf coming.
Was there a wolf there at that time?
No, but Peter Reith informed me there was a wolf.
Where was he saying the wolf was?
He said the wolf was in the water.
A wolf in the water? What would a wolf be doing in the water? Wolves aren't found in the water are they?
These wolves were.
According to Peter Reith.
That's right.
And then it turned out they weren't there at all?
As it turned out, yes.
What happened next?

George Bush announced he was going to conduct a war on Iraq.

What did you do when that happened?

I did what I was told.

Yes, but what did you actually say?

I said I'd seen a wolf.

Did you yell this out?

Well, I went on television and said that I'd seen a wolf.

Another wolf?

Yes.

This time in Iraq?

Yes.

You'd seen a wolf in Iraq. And how would you have seen a wolf in Iraq?

I didn't actually see it. George saw it.

And how did you know George had seen a wolf?

He rang me up and shouted 'wolf' down the phone.

'Wolf in Iraq'?

Yes.

So now you'd said you'd seen two wolves.

The one in the water and the one in Iraq, yes.

And how many had you actually seen?

Strictly speaking?

Yes.

I hadn't seen any.

And then what happened?

Then we got attacked by a wolf.

This was in Bali?

Yes, that's right.

And did you see that coming?

No. We had no warning of any kind.

And what were you doing at the time?

I was very busy at the time.

Doing what?

I was on television trying to describe the wolf I'd seen in Iraq.

The wolf you *hadn't* seen in Iraq.

Yes, well, both of them really.

Which both of them?

The wolf I hadn't seen in Iraq and the wolf I hadn't seen in the water.

So whose fault is all this, do you think?

The wolf's. Let's be quite clear about that.

Of course, Mr Howard.

It was all the wolf's fault. LOOK OUT!

THE MOST REVEREND PETER HOLLINGWORTH, GOVERNOR-GENERAL OF AUSTRALIA

In which the Mad Hatter makes an appearance.

Bishop Hollingworth, thanks for your time.
It's very good to be here and thank you very, very much for inviting
me. It's a great pleasure to be here.
Good. Would you like a cup of tea?
Yes, if you've got the kettle on, I'll have a quick one, yes. Have you got
any shortbread?
Shortbread?
The little finger ones? I love those. Could I have a couple?
Two?
Just two, thank you.
Two shortbreads, thanks.
Lovely, I adore those.
They are good, I agree.
Mmm.
Your Eminence, you've been in the news a bit lately, haven't you?
I have, your ordinariness. Yes, I've never seen so much publicity!
You like publicity?
Well, it's a public job. I think it's incumbent to make it visible.
But you enjoy the job, don't you?
I do, I'm enjoying the job a great deal. I mean, everything is nice at the
moment. Beautiful weather, for example.
Nice weather.
Oh, yes, ideal. No rain. Wonderful summer we're having.
Drought. There's a drought.
Where?
In Australia.
In Australia?

Yes.

Harry, give the Queen a ring, will you? Tell her we're having trout.

No, a drought. Drought.

There's been a drought? Harry, tell her she better be quick. There won't be a lot of it.

Your Grace, have you completed your renovations?

Very nearly. Just a couple of little loose ends, but we're very nearly there and we're very, very pleased with the result.

And what remains to be done?

Just a few tiny things. The tap fittings, for example, didn't really work with the bathroom.

So you got some new tap fittings?

No, we got a new bathroom.

And what else?

Oh, a problem with carpets, for example.

Really?

They weren't expensive enough.

So what do you do in these cases, Your Eminence? Do you get more expensive ones?

Yes, you can get some very, very expensive ones these days, yes.

Where do you get them from?

Overseas. We got this one in France.

Whereabouts?

It's on the left-hand end of Europe. It's a big joint. Gaul.

I know where France is. Whereabouts in France?

A place called 'Bayoo', I think it was.

Bayeux?

That's right, Bayeux. It's not really a carpet. It's more of a rug.

It's a tapestry. The Bayeux tapestry.

It's a tapestry! I couldn't have put it better myself. It's a bit thin actually. I think the dogs have given it a bit of a shagging.

So, apart from that, Your Excellency, are there any other problems with the vice-regal accommodation?

As I say, we're very nearly there with the renovations. We're just waiting on a little bit of marble for the light fittings.

Why would you have marble light fittings?

They're Italian light fittings.

What does that mean?

It means you need Italian marble. You can't have Italian light fittings, can you…

Without the Italian marble? Of course not. Your Lordship, what else remains to be done on the apartment?

Oh, there's a list somewhere. Speaking from memory, I think there's some bombing to be done.

Where?

Iraq, I think the bloke said. *(Loud crashing sound.)* What was that?

I don't know.

Harry, I think one of the Whiteleys has gone again. It will be the third one near the door. That's right. No, up the other way—it's a woman.

Your Eminence, thanks for your time.

I'll just have one more quick cup of tea, sonny, and then I really must go.

THE HON. JOHN HOWARD, PRIME MINISTER OF AUSTRALIA

In which we apologise for a slight technical problem.

Mr Howard, thanks for your time.
Good evening. Very nice of you to invite me on the program.
Mr Howard, looking at the size of the demonstrations against the war in Iraq…
Can I just make the point that not everybody was on those demonstrations.
Not everybody could be. They were only on in certain places. Not everybody could get to them. My point about…
No, more importantly, my point, Bryan, is that, in this country, there are a great many citizens who do not find it necessary to stand on some rooftop somewhere and scream out their semi-literate opinions for the whole bloody world to listen to.
You mean Australians like to keep their views to themselves?
I do. I think there's a manly and rather admirable kind of Anzac, muscular Christian quality to a lot of people in this country, such that they SHUT UP!
The majority of people in the country oppose the war.
You're wilfully misunderstanding my point.
I don't think I'm misunderstanding anything.
Let me put it this way—I spent last weekend talking to people on exactly this issue as well. And of all the people I spoke to last weekend, not one of them, Bryan, agreed with those demonstrators.
Not one?
Not one.
Where were you last weekend?
I was in Washington, Bryan. I'm the Australian prime minister. *(His voice is not in sync with his mouth.)*
Sorry, Mr Howard, hang on, it seems you're slightly out of sync.
No I'm not. Don't be ridiculous. What do you mean I'm out of sync?

I think you're a bit out of sync.

(He is now miles out of synch.) I'm not out of sync, Bryan.

Shane, I think Mr Howard's out of sync.

Don't be ridiculous, Bryan. I'm not out of sync at all.

You don't think you're out of sync?

I know bloody well I'm not out of sync.

How can you tell? I think you are.

Bryan, I am sick of people telling me I am out of sync.

Producer: Yes. He's out of sync, Bryan. Hang on, we're working on it.

Who's that?

They're working on it, Mr Howard.

They're working on what?

On the problem.

Who are they?

Producer: Can he speak faster and try to catch up to himself?

Hello? Who are these people?

Mr Howard, could you say a few words for us?

Sure, what about?

Anything. Tell us about the GST.

We will never introduce a GST into Australia, ever.

Yes, he's definitely out of sync, Shane. You're definitely out of sync, Mr Howard.

I'm not out of sync at all.

Producer: Ask him to speak a bit faster and catch up with himself.

Could you speak a bit faster?

Want me to do some fast talking?

Yes, try and catch up with yourself.

(Speaks quickly.) If people don't like what I'm doing, Bryan, they can vote me out at the next election.

Hang on, no, that's not working.

Fast talking normally works. It's been a bit of a stalwart for me. What do you mean it's not working?

Because the election will be after the war.

Exactly, of course, Bryan. I'm not a complete idiot.

No, you're out of sync again.

Producer: He's completely out of sync, Bryan. Wrap it up.

Wrap who up?

Thanks for coming in, Mr Howard.

Can I just thank all Australians for their support?

Definitely out of sync.

THE HON. PETER COSTELLO, TREASURER OF AUSTRALIA

In which our driver is pulled over and asked to produce a current licence.

Mr Costello, thanks for your time.
Hello, Trevor, nice to be with you.

Bryan.
Bryan, very good to be with you.

Mr Costello, Australia has a deficit of $11.6 billion.
Yes.

It seems like a hell of a lot.
I don't think there's any question about that. It's a very large amount of money.

Mr Costello, as an economist…
I'm actually not, technically speaking, an economist.

Well, OK, just in terms of accounting then.
I'm not an accountant either. Can I make that point?

Well, what are you?
I'm the Federal Treasurer of Australia.

But what are your qualifications for being the treasurer?
I was offered the job, and you're normally thought to be one out and one back if you've got the gig, so I took it.

Mr Costello, this is the biggest deficit in our history.
Yes, it's not insubstantial.

It's bigger than the Keating black hole. It's bigger than the Beazley black hole.
Yes, indeed.

It's billions of dollars bigger than any of these.
It's very, very big indeed.

What are you going to call this deficit? They all have names, don't they?
We've given some thought as to what we might call this one.

What are you going to call it?

We think the 'Drought black hole'.

Not the 'Costello black hole'?

No, no, no. Listen very carefully to what I'm saying. We think the 'Drought black hole' is what we're going to call this one.

What about all the money people are paying in taxes? Where's all the money going? The GST is in. Prices are going up. You must be making a fortune.

Yes, nobody could be more acutely aware of these things.

Oil is going up, food prices are going up.

We have had some costs...

You may well have.

We have had some costs, significant costs.

But this government is taking in more money than any time in history.

I repeat—we have had costs.

So where's it all going?

It's gone on the things that we're spending the money on.

Like what?

We've had an asylum-seeker crisis on our hands, for example.

Come on, when was that?

I'd be speaking from memory.

Well, go on, try and remember.

It was just before the last election. Remember Peter Reith?

Yeah.

Well, it was about ten minutes before he resigned.

But that was a while ago. You must have been spending billions since then.

Yes, we've had quite a lot of costs.

Mr Costello, I'll ask you again—what is it being spent on?

Well, health, education, welfare, aged care, not on these areas—these are areas where we have made savings.

Has the budget in the defence area gone up?

I don't know that 'up' adequately describes what's happened to the defence budget.

What is it at the moment?

It's out at the moment having an extension put on it, but I can't go into details.

What sort of extension?

We're having a warehouse popped on the back of the defence budget to put some of the zeros in—there are quite a lot of zeros there. And we're having a little terrace cantilevered out over the lawn so there's a view. There's quite a lot of expense in that area.

Mr Costello, will there be anything else in the budget?

Yes, the warehouse will have to be paid for. Warehouses don't fall off trees. We're going to have to build this thing and it's going to cost money.

Mr Costello, thanks for your time.

Health, education and welfare…

You mentioned all those.

…Aboriginal affairs and aged care—these are the areas we're making savings, valuable savings for the Australian people.

Mr Costello, thank you very much.

Shut up.

THE HON. JOHN HOWARD, ALEXANDER DOWNER AND ROBERT HILL

In which desperate measures are sometimes taken in order to elicit information.

Gentlemen, let's check those buzzers.
John Howard: (*Low-pitched buzzer sounds.*)
Alexander Downer: (*High-pitched buzzer sounds.*)
Robert Hill: (*'Star Spangled Banner' sounds.*)
OK. First question: What is the exact military situation in Iraq at this present moment?
(*Long pause.*)
Anyone?
(*Long pause.*)
Do you want to check those buzzers?
John Howard: (*Low-pitched buzzer sounds.*)
Alexander Downer: (*High-pitched buzzer sounds.*)
Robert Hill: (*'Star Spangled Banner' sounds.*)
Good. OK, let's move on. We'll go to another question. The purpose of the war in Iraq is to remove Saddam Hussein from the leadership— buzzers ready? Where is Saddam Hussein?
(*Long pause.*)
(*High-pitched buzzer sounds.*)
Alexander Downer?
Somewhere in Iraq, Bryan?
Can you be more specific?
No, I'm sorry, I can't.
No. OK. Let's move on to another one. What is the planned duration of the war?
(*Long pause.*)
Anyone? How long will the war last?
(*Low-pitched buzzer sounds.*)
Mr Howard?

Can we phone a friend?

No. Just check your buzzers again if you wouldn't mind.

John Howard: *(Low-pitched buzzer sounds.)*

Alexander Downer: *(High-pitched buzzer sounds.)*

Robert Hill: *('Star Spangled Banner' sounds.)*

Good. We'll move on to another question. On the issue of postwar reconstruction—has anyone spoken to the Iraqis? *(Repeats the question.)* **Has anyone spoken to the Iraqis?**

(Long pause.)

(Low-pitched buzzer sounds.)

Mr Howard?

Can you repeat the question please, Bryan.

Yes. On the question of postwar reconstruction, has anyone spoken to the Iraqis?

(High-pitched buzzer sounds.)

Mr Downer?

Can you repeat the question again, Bryan?

Look, I think we'll move on. Here's one you'll all get. Ready? What is a crumbling operation?

('Star Spangled Banner' sounds.)

Robert Hill?

That's where you kill a lot of people and blow stuff up.

(Fourth person joins the panel.)

Excuse me. Hello, who are you?

I'm Donald Rumsfeld.

How can we help you?

(Buzzers sound in unison and continue forever. All contestants stand.)

THE HON. KIM BEAZLEY, LABOR BACKBENCHER

In which we are delighted to receive a visit from an old friend.

Mr Beazley, thanks for your time.

Well, thank you. It's very nice to be here and thank you for the invitation.

Yes, nice to see you again.

We have met before, haven't we? You're, um…

Bryan Dawe.

You're Bryan.

That's right. I interviewed you the first time you got beaten by John Howard.

I remember.

And then I interviewed you the second time you got beaten by John Howard.

Ah, yes. I did recognise you. I just couldn't put a name to it.

Now, I've read this piece in the *Bulletin* and you obviously think that if you can regain the leadership of the Opposition you can get beaten again.

I think I have it in me to be beaten a third time. I've had a bit of time to think about this on the backbench.

You have.

I'm not exactly putting my hand up.

You're not exactly holding it down either.

Well, it's all speculative.

You're taking a bit of criticism, though, aren't you?

To a degree. I mean, one or two people have, yes, cleared their throats on the matter.

Because it is Simon Crean's turn to get thrashed.

Technically it's Simon's turn to be beaten by John Howard, yes.

He does have a point.

He does have a point, I agree.

I mean, his point is that he's never been beaten by John Howard and so why should he let you get murdered a third time?

Because I'm so bloody good at it. I've been beaten handsomely twice by John Howard. As you yourself have just said, Simon's never been beaten by John Howard.

Crean's argument is that he's not going so badly. His popularity is at minus 27.

Yes, but that could come up again. At least with me you *know* you're going to get belted.

But it is his job to be beaten, isn't it, at the moment?

Yes, technically he is in that role.

In fact, you gave him the job. You stood aside at the last election.

I did, but he's such a novice. I've been humiliated by John Howard twice.

I think we accept that you've got a gift for it. But does it really ultimately matter who gets beaten?

I suppose it doesn't matter as long as somebody gets beaten.

From a party point of view?

From a party point of view, I suppose it doesn't much matter, yes.

As long as you don't win?

As long as we keep the party out of office.

So why not leave Crean alone? Let him have a go.

Well, it's just that I miss it so much. Every few years I used to get beaten by John Howard.

Sure, but if you look at it this way, at least you can say you helped, Mr Beazley.

I suppose I cannot unreasonably make that claim, yes.

I mean, you're the one who refused to take a stand on the asylum seekers.

That's very true, that is true.

You trebled the Green vote.

I did an enormous amount for the Greens when I ran the Labor Party.

And he'd have no show of being humiliated the way he is at the moment if it hadn't been for the work you'd put in earlier.

That's very, very nice of you to say that, Bryan.

Well, that's just what I'm thinking, you know.

Well, thank you. Thank you very much.

It's a pleasure.

I feel better just having talked to you about it.

Well, any time.

It's a bit rough out there, but to get someone who understands, it's just great.

That's quite OK, Mr Beazley.

THE HON. JOHN HOWARD, PRIME MINISTER OF AUSTRALIA

In which the tricky matter of health is once again successfully avoided.

Mr Howard, thanks for your time.

Good evening, and thank you for inviting me on the program.

I wonder if I could ask you about health.

Certainly, yes, never better, Bryan. Fit as a buck rat.

No, I didn't mean your health. I mean health generally.

Someone else's health? Who gives a toss…Oh! I see—as a concept, as a portfolio?

That's right.

(Off.) Get Kay will you please? Kay Patterson.

I would like to talk to you specifically about Medicare, Mr Howard, because you said you would never change it.

I didn't, Kay did. *(Off.)* Get Kay will you please, quickly. The change has cropped up.

Who appointed Kay, Mr Howard?

Kay was an excellent appointment and I did that personally, that was my idea.

Well I'd like to talk to you then.

I'm really more in the area of highly successful international warfare. I will give it a belt for you, obviously, but…

Mr Howard, what was the problem with Medicare?

As I understand it, Bryan, the problem was that people were in some cases beginning to understand aspects of it.

People understood the health system?

That's always the risk, Bryan.

People knowing how to use it?

Yes.

Mr Howard, how can people use it properly if they don't understand how it works?

Exactly. Well spotted, Bryan.

I mean really, Mr Howard, isn't it simple enough? A person goes to the doctor, and that's it.

Well, that's rather a crude analysis. Who pays the doctor, for example?

The government. The doctor charges the fee to Medicare.

So the patient goes to a doctor and doesn't pay the doctor at all?

No, the patient has already paid. Medicare is funded through our money, through taxpayers' money.

No, that would never work.

Why not?

Where's the gap? How will insurance companies make a quid in any of this?

Well they're not making a quid now. They're losing a fortune.

If they did, though, where is the gap? Who is going to fund the gap?

What gap?

The gap that prevents the system from working, Bryan. Who's going to fund it?

Mr Howard, why should there be a gap at all?

You can't tell doctors what to charge. We as a government can't tell doctors what to charge. They're not civil servants, doctors, and they don't want to be.

Mr Howard, patients don't want to be paying an arm and a leg to go to a doctor.

Well, they can go to another doctor, Bryan. That is the glorious choice they have in this system.

OK, Mr Howard. So what do you do? Let's say you've got a broken arm.

You've got a broken arm. Obviously cradle your broken arm, get to a phone and ring an actuary.

An actuary?

Yes. You're going to need an actuary because you need to know the best combination of your medical needs, your insurance capabilities and then extrapolate that in terms of your tax position over a sustained period.

Mr Howard, your needs are that you've got a broken arm.

Let's not be distracted by your particular problem.

Leave the medical problem aside?

You want to ask me about the system itself, don't you?

I do, but you only come in contact with the system when you have a medical problem.

And whatever your medical problem is, Bryan, what we want is that when you turn up with it, we've got a system that we've devised that's firing on all six.

But Mr Howard, don't you see, you're trying to get the system to work for you, not for the patient.

But we're not ready for the patient.

Why not?

Because he's probably still talking to the actuary.

He's got a broken arm, Mr Howard.

(*Off.*) Get Kay in here quickly, will you? Patient presenting with delusions…

Mr Howard, I haven't got delusions.

…thinks the health system ought to work. No, I'll keep him talking in the meantime, but tell her to be quick.

Hello, Bryan.

THE HON. PETER COSTELLO, TREASURER OF AUSTRALIA

In which we find it necessary to have a word with one of the boys.

Mr Costello, thanks for your time.
Very good to be with you, Bryan, very good indeed.
Well, you're out selling the Budget. What's the reaction from the flock?
It's going very well. The flock are pleased and I think it's broadly seen as a very sensible and responsible Budget.
And they'd have to be happy with a tax cut?
Yes, you put $513 per week in their kick and they won't complain too much, will they?
Who is getting that again?
If you're a forty-five-year-old male politician from Kooyong with a wife and family, you're getting $513 in your pocket per week extra—more than under the twelve Labor Budgets put together.
The Iraqi war cost Australia a lot, didn't it?
Well, I think you've got to face facts, Bryan. If you're going to invade another country, it's going to belt your projections around a bit.
Now, the higher education package, can you explain that to me?
Certainly. At the moment, the way the system is, and we're just adding just a mere 30 per cent to this, if you go to a university there are two ways you can pay. You can pay full fees, Bryan—
Up front?
Yes, full fees, that is.
And how much does that cost?
Well, it depends on what course you do.
Say a three-year course?
Yes, a nice little bottom of the range product. About 40 gorillas.
Gordon Bennett!
Or else—What's his name?
Gordon Bennett.

Gordon could perhaps pay using the old H.E.C.S. method, which we're replacing with another one—

Lay-by?

Yes, lay-by, yes. Nice easy terms, see one of our friendly staff, Bryan.

And how does Gordon pay it back?

He pays it back later when he's earning a quid and kicking on rather well.

And you charge interest?

Only a bit.

So what would he owe on that?

Well, if Gordon paid this back over perhaps five years, we might be into him for about 45K.

Gordon Bennett! What if he did law or medicine?

Yes, by all means. Are his parents doctors or lawyers?

I don't know.

He won't be doing law or medicine if his parents aren't doctors or lawyers.

So the only people who can do law or medicine are people who have parents who are doctors and lawyers?

Well, if we've got the projections right, Bryan, on those figures, that's where the landing lights are, yes—

So why make them do the course in the first place?

I see. If they're the only people who can do the course, why bother running the course!

They'd pick it up at home, wouldn't they?

Good point, Bryan. Of course we'd have to subsidise that, but we'd be able to do that with the money we're yanking out of the education budget—Good point.

What about the people whose parents aren't doctors and lawyers? There must be a few of those?

People who go to university and have not got a parent who is either a doctor or a lawyer?

Yes.

Yes. Well, have you read the Budget documents?

Yes.

Well, they're going to be nurses and teachers, aren't they?

Gordon Bennett.

Let me be clear, Byran. We're not opposed to the mongrel class going to university, they're just not getting into the professions.

And what's called again, this scheme?

H.E.L.P.

THE HON. PHILIP RUDDOCK, MINISTER FOR IMMIGRATION AND MULTICULTURAL AND INDIGENOUS AFFAIRS

In which we become extremely interested and impressed.

Mr Ruddock, thanks for your time.
What I will say with regard to that is that the department and indeed officers in the department charged with…

Sorry, Mr Ruddock, I haven't asked you anything yet.
What I will say with regard to the procedural matter you raise, and it is a procedural matter, is that there are guidelines for the answering of questions…

Mr Ruddock, excuse me. I'm thanking you for coming in.
What I will say with regard to that…

Mr Ruddock, I haven't actually asked you any questions yet.
What I will say with regard to the procedural matter, and I repeat, is I will be acting at all times in accordance with the guidelines…

Mr Ruddock? Mr Ruddock?
…for discussing the issues you have raised and issues evolving from the issues you have raised…

Mr Ruddock? Mr Ruddock, how are you?
What I will say with regard to the wellbeing of any individual or individuals is that those discussions will be undertaken at an appropriate time…

By the appropriate authority?
…by, as you say, the appropriate authority.

Did you enjoy the cricket?
What I will say with regard to the cricket, in so far as it is an issue at all…

Did you enjoy it?
I would like to be given the opportunity to respond to your question.

Certainly.

What I would say with regard both to cricket and to sporting contests of any other kind, be they games or contests of the hand and eye…

Good grief.

…contests of speed, of strength or even of mental agility…

Or a combination of the two.

…particularly where they occur in combination…

I think I'll just keep going. I'll see if I can get an answer.

…what I would say is that in so far as they are issues, and they are not issues, this is not new information…

God, you are boring.

…and what I would say with regard to these issues, and these are not, as I say, new issues, is that my ability to answer these questions is beyond question.

Yes, or any other question.

…or any other question of any kind.

Yes.

My job, and you must understand it, is to ensure that the issues you raise and issues involving…

Does he have an off switch?

…those issues you raise will not appear in tomorrow's newspaper. And if they do appear in tomorrow's newspaper, it is further my undertaking to ensure that they do not appear in the front section of the newspaper or in a prominent section of the newspaper or a well-read section of the newspaper.

Mr Ruddock, would you mind going away?

Good, I got away with it, Harry.

THE HON. PETER COSTELLO, TREASURER OF AUSTRALIA

In which we find it necessary to have a word with one of the boys.

Sit down, Peter. *(Peter sits down.)* **What's the matter?**

Nothing.

Can I ask you a few questions?

All right.

You don't seem very happy.

I'm all right.

What happened?

Nothing.

Come on, I heard all about it. What happened?

Johnny wouldn't give me a go on the bike. He'll never give me a go on the bike now.

Did he say he would give you a go?

Yes, but he won't. He'll be on it forever. He'll never get off it now.

Hang on. What did he actually say?

He said he'd give me a go.

Didn't he say he'd *think about* giving you a go?

Yes, but he won't. I'll never get a go on the bike now.

Look, I'm sure he'll give you a go.

When?

When he's ready.

I want a go now. He said I could have a go now.

Johnny's having a go now, and he's pretty good at it. I've seen him going past my office a few times.

You should see him when he's not going past your office. He doesn't even tell the truth. He tells big whoppers about what's going on.

Johnny doesn't tell the truth? What are these big whoppers he's been telling?

If I tell you what the big whoppers are, he'll *never* let me have a go on the bike.

But if you don't tell us what the big whoppers are, you'll be helping him tell the big whoppers.

Yes I know. Bloody Johnny.

He's snookered you a bit here, hasn't he?

I hate Johnny.

Come on, you don't hate him. You're just a bit angry.

I'm bloody furious.

We all get angry from time to time. Look on the plus side. Johnny lets you play with the accounts, and there are people who say you're really not very good at that.

I only got one thing wrong.

Yes, but it was rather a big thing, wasn't it?

No, I only put the wrong price in for Telstra.

But you could have got the right price, couldn't you?

How?

It was in the paper, wasn't it, Peter?

I didn't have a paper.

So what did you do?

I made a price up.

So it looked as if there was a surplus?

Johnny told me to do that. That was Johnny's idea to have a surplus.

Bloody Johnny, I hate Johnny.

Look, let John have his turn and then when he's finished, you'll get to have a go. And I'm sure you'll be very good at it too.

I should have had a go a long time ago.

You'll have a go.

Thanks for coming to see me.

That's all right. Feel a bit better now?

Not really.

THE HON. JOHN HOWARD, PRIME MINISTER OF AUSTRALIA

In which, when things get tough, at a difficult age, we struggle to be fair.

John, John, John. What are we going to do with you? I've had a look at the work you've handed in. It's not very good is it?

It's all right.

Who wrote this?

I did.

Are you sure?

Yes.

Who really wrote it?

I did.

Is this your handwriting?

Yes.

Come on, John. This is typed.

Oh, yes. I typed it.

Where did you get this paper?

I bought it.

It's fax paper.

No, it isn't.   haven't they?

Yes, it is. Someone else has done this and faxed it

No they haven't.   n eagle at the top

John, it's got a US military letterhead on it. Th
here.

Oh, I did that.

How did you do that?

Derwents.

Who's George?

I don't know any George.

Look. The point is this is not you ssay. We don't want you handing
in other people's work. The pro lem is not that you're fooling the

system, John. The danger here is that *you're fooling yourself.*

Can I go the toilet?

No, you can wait till I've finished. (*Reads.***) 'Iraq. By John Howard'.**

How do you spell 'John'?

J-O-H-N.

That's not what you've got here. What are WMDs?

Weapons of mass destruction.

What are they?

Bombs and stuff.

Bombs and stuff?

Yes.

Where are they?

In Iraq.

Whereabouts? You don't say where they are. Where are your references?

dog ate my footnotes.

you have to present some evidence. No-one is going to be

nced by this. Where are these things? In the ground? Up trees?

now.

Th 't know, it shouldn't be in here.

If the en.

they're t n how do you know they're there? You can't just *say*

Yes you ca

You're going

You're biased. to do this again. I'm not accepting this.

I'm not biased, Joh

here. It just doesn't m trying to understand what you're saying

George said it did. nse.

Well, George is a very silly

Bloody George.

THE HON. JOHN HOWARD, PRIME MINISTER OF AUSTRALIA

Mr Howard, is there anything else you'd like to add, before we go?
Did I thank the media?
Yes, you did that earlier.
Could I thank them again? I don't mean to go on about it but I'm reminded, in reading through what we've done, that we, as a government, simply couldn't have got away wi...
...achieved.
...that we simply couldn't have achieved the things we've got away wi...
...the things you've achieved.
That we simply couldn't have achieved the things we've managed to achieve if it hadn't been for the free ride we've had from some of the more favourably unbiased elements in the media.
One thing I wonder, Mr Howard, as I see history playing itself out in these pages, is where you think we're going, as a nation?
Let me say something about that because it's an extremely important question.
I ask because our country seems to have changed a great deal under your guidance.
Well, we're evolving all the time. What sort of changes do you mean?
We've gone from being an inclusive society to being told by our own government to fear difference.
I see.
We were a respected international peacemaker. Now we're a terrorist target.
Yes, I see what you mean. I think...
We have introduced changes to the tax system in order to free people from the burden of over-taxation.
That's correct. We've done that.
And we find ourselves now having to put away a day a month to

do our tax. On a computer.

Pay an accountant. It'll be a lot faster.

The government's tax take has increased by billions. And Australia has a *deficit*.

I take your point.

Nothing has been done on the environment because you spent a fortune on a war in Iraq. Our own biggest river system is destroyed. Health and education are in crisis.

Look, I understand what you're saying.

You have brought about enormous change in this country.

I accept that. The question is, 'Was this the purpose behind my actions, or was it simply a consequence of them?'

Is there a difference?

There's a difference, for example, between orchestrating Pauline Hanson's rise to prominence on the one hand and going to the cricket on the other.

You've gone off the point a bit there, Mr Howard. You're trying to draw a more subtle distinction than that, aren't you?

Yes, I beg your pardon. Your observation is an acute one. There is a difference between running her campaign on the one hand, and creating the atmosphere in which it might thrive on the other.

But in either case you would be engaging in action designed to move Australia to the right by encouraging ignorant racist paranoia.

My point is that there's a difference between doing something and letting it happen. Take the Tampa crisis. I've been accused of precipitating that crisis simply because I didn't avert it.

You milked it.

Did I thank the media, incidentally?

Yes, you've done that.

I don't think we could have done that without the…

Mr Howard, you might not have caused the crisis but you manipulated the extent and effect of it.

But I didn't *cause* it!

Do you see a distinction between planning a robbery and conducting it?

Of course. There's an obvious difference between a senior executive position and the role of a common thief.

I notice, Mr Howard, we seem to have grown out of our sycophantic dependence on England.

Great days. Halcyon days. Days of very fond memory.

But it was colonial, wasn't it?

It was. In the end it was time we grew up. We are a more mature nation now.

Are we?

Yes. We have a sycophantic dependence on America now.

So we're really getting somewhere, as a sovereign nation?

Absolutely. The minute free trade comes in we'll be out of trouble.

When will that be?

I might say Australia is better prepared for the advent of free trade than any other country on earth.

And what exactly will happen?

Trade will be completely free. Trade barriers will come down. We've already dismantled ours.

But our farmers can't sell their produce into the American market.

Not yet, but they'll be able to when the trade barriers come down.

Didn't you just say we'd dismantled them?

We have, but the Americans need to dismantle theirs too.

It takes two to tango.

That is my understanding.

Will we sell manufactured goods?

No, we don't have a manufacturing sector.

Really? Why not.

We dismantled our trade barriers. We're ready to roll the minute free trade comes in.

Mr Howard, thanks for everything.

It's always a pleasure. Can I take a moment to thank the media?

You've done that, Mr Howard.

Are you sure?

I've never been surer of anything in my life.